Praise for *H*

"*Hold Space* represents a wonderful compilation of powerful, accessible reflections and life strategies told in a compassionate and wise voice. Michelle Rose Kennedy's work struck a deep chord relative to my own healing journey and that of so many therapy clients over the years. The affirmations are fantastic. I felt my heart open and my respiration slow when I read each one of them!"

—Deborah Sosin, LICSW, mindfulness therapist;
author of *Charlotte and the Quiet Place*
and *Breaking Free of Addiction*

Finding inspiration to enrich our soul and balance our emotions is a never-ending journey. Light-giver Michelle Rose Kennedy has successfully managed that in *Hold Space: Affirmations & Meditations for Healing & Loving Yourself*, just as the title suggests. Not only does Michelle write candidly about her own experiences she provides actual, practical movements, phrases and words that will help propel you to tap into your own inner opportunities, greatness, and healing, leaving behind the negativity that oft haunts oneself in self-examination. *Hold Space* offers the reader practical habits that can help (you) tackle life's biggest obstacles and find new ways to show appreciation and love for people and the world around us. *Hold Space* is a true, usable guide motivating the reader in an easy, friendly way, allowing them to get imaginative, creative, and kind towards oneself. I highly recommend picking up this gem for your own bookshelf or as a great gift for those around you who are struggling – which in reality is each and every one of us at any given time!

—"Malibu Sue" Sue McCann, Radio Personality/DJ; Actress;
Key Contributor to the Documentary, *Dare to be Different*

As a therapist, my role is to hold space for others. I can now offer **Hold Space**, Michelle Rose Kennedy's book as an additional tool beyond the therapy room, that allows people to feel held and self-heal through each affirmation. Michelle's relatable, authentic, and down to earth voice is heard throughout this book, allowing words of wisdom to be easily absorbed. I appreciate that this book provides clear definitions of new-age concepts, interwoven with personal stories that made me feel connected. I love that I can read this book by topic that resonates with me that day and receive an affirmation or meditation that I need in that moment for healing!"

—Kelly Lennon-Martucci, LCSW, RYT;
"40 Under 40 Rising Star" New York Non-Profit Media, 2016
Emerging Leader Award NASW, 2014

"Hold Space is a beautiful read. The chapter on forgiveness resonated with me most. I got some much-needed sustenance from Michelle Rose Kennedy's voice, and the clear, concise messages."

—Robert Burke Warren, Author of *Perfectly Broken*;
writer for *Hudson Valley One*; Singer/Songwriter

HOLD SPACE

Affirmations & Meditations
for Healing & Loving Yourself

by
Michelle Rose Kennedy

My Reiki Healer, LLC

Library of Congress Cataloging-in-Publication Data
Kennedy, Michelle Rose
Hold Space: Affirmations & Meditations
for Healing & Loving Yourself; First Edition
  1.   Self-Help Techniques—Non-Fiction
  2.   Spirituality—Non-Fiction
  3.   Mind and Body—Non-Fiction
Cover Art by Chanel Mülhaupt
ISBN (ebook): 978-1-7371265-0-8
ISBN (paperback): 978-1-7371265-2-2

Published by My Reiki Healer, LLC
Printed in the United States of America

*This book is dedicated to
my husband, Greg and our children, Devon Jane and Korben
and to my Aunt Cathy,
who I felt with me throughout the creative process*

Hold Space *is also dedicated to anyone suffering,
all the survivors of trauma, heartbreak, grief, dysfunctional families,
or just feeling different. Embrace your difference.
You are worthy and completely lovable!*

"You are the universe expressing itself as a human for a little while."
– Eckhart Tolle

Table of Contents

ACKNOWLEDGEMENTS

A lot of life experiences and people go into a book, no matter if it's fiction or nonfiction. Each and every one of my experiences and every single relationship, client, teacher, and student has shaped me and the contents of this book. I worked tirelessly to include everything that was meant to be part of this book and I'm proud of how it turned out. I take a very "no regrets" approach to life and I have a small, but loyal and sometimes brutally honest, support team around me. It's important to have people around that will give it to you straight and call you on your bullshit. We all have bullshit talk that comes out of us or that we feed ourselves based on fear. The straightshooters in my life are the ones I value most, because I too have a reputation of being straightforward and sometimes unfiltered. Some may see this as a flaw. I believe every flaw has the potential to be a gift. I am exactly who I am and that's okay. I don't want to be anyone else and I find it challenging, at times, to fit into the mold of what society wants women, healers, mothers, people to be.

I have been through enough in life to have earned the right to be me, unapologetically. living unapologetically does not mean I'm a bitch that never says, "I'm sorry." If I hurt someone along the way, I am compassionate enough to admit it and apologize.

Hold Space is not a memoir, but I felt very strongly about thanking my past experiences for shaping me into the person I am today. If it had been any different, I would not be the me I am right now. I would not feel the same sense of strength, empathy, or call to help other people heal and love themselves too.

As a child, I had recurring nightmares about war and had such bad asthma that I was called "trigger lungs" by the many doctors who got to know me at the local emergency room. No judgment. No regrets. My illness exposed me to a diverse population of people. Doctors, nurse, and patients of all different backgrounds were at the hospitals and low-income clinics I frequented. As awful as it was to be in and out of the hospital since elementary school, I learned many life lessons and had unique experiences that shaped my world views.

My first suicidal thought was age 10, the year my lung collapsed. At 13, I wrote my first suicidal poem. My teen years improved when I got my driver's license and decided to become a vegetarian. That was my teenage rebellion; it doesn't sound like much, but everyone in the family was against it. Again, no anger, judgment or regrets. I was passionate about something and was willing to fight the powers of my parents to do what I knew was right for me.

After high school, I picked a diverse, local community college, not because I didn't have the grades, but because I wanted diversity in my life. I didn't want to go to a white-washed school like all the ones I grew up with. I wanted to be with the people I spent time with in the hospitals and clinics. I met lots of people and made lots of friends. I had bought my own new car, had a job and had a life of my own and was healthier. At age 19, I was raped. It was the absolute worst moment of my life. That tragedy sent me to my bottom. A lot more happened in the next few years, but this book is for you and the key is that at the bottom, I learned, you can only rise up! I am eternally grateful for the few good friends who took me to psych services at school. That was the beginning of my healing.

I have so much gratitude for my husband, Greg Schweizer. I thank him for pushing me to buckle down and write. From early on in our relationship, our psychic medium friend, Jeffrey Wands, said that "writer" was written on my soul. Greg never let me forget that. He also encouraged me to slow down and not rush this book out there. Greg so often holds the mirror for me to see myself as I truly am and to rise to my own power. He is the creative and technical force behind the guided meditations that supplement this book. His is the only ear I trust with such things. I am eternally grateful that I married a creative partner, because our children took the best of our collective DNA and are the most creative and incredible people I know.

Teenagers will always give it to you straight. Our daughter is a writer and musician. If Devon Jane gives me a writing note, I'm listening. I trust her as a wordsmith and both of our children have a keen artistic eye. Our son is the brooding artist and what he says may be sharp, but it is pure wisdom. He has been drawing and sketching since he could hold a crayon. And though most of Korben's creative juice now goes to culinary arts, he still has that critical eye. Both of them were essential to my cover art decisions and revisions.

I am grateful to my grandmother, Rita, who bought me my first typewriter at age 10, who insisted I use it if she was going to spend $15 at a yard sale; boy did I get a lot of use out of it!

I thank my parents, Rita and Thomas for bringing me into this world, all the lessons, and keeping me alive through those sick years. I cannot imagine growing up without my sisters, Amy and Cheryl; thanks for the comradery as well as the rivalry.

Thank you to Rosemarie Nania, who took the time to read the whole book, prior to edits and before I was ready to show the world. Thanks to Kelly Wollschlager has been cheering me on for as long as I've known him and shared his wisdom and words throughout the process and pitch. Matt Burlingame, who has been writing for as long as we've known each other and encouraged me to keep at it, thank you! I am indebted to Melissa Anders for inviting me to join her in Leonie Dawson's "40 Days to a Finished Book". Eileen Schellhorn, Jon Oz, Karla Torres, Matty Taher, Brian Di Marino, Ilene Rubin Hellman, and my beloved Starseeds (1212): Shereen Balhetchet, Legera Danielides, Justina Del Rio, and Elise Del Rio may not realize how important they were to the creative process, but I am appreciative of their presence in my life and all the feedback they gave.

That brings me to the cover artist. I found Chanel Mülhaupt on Instagram of all places. After a mishap with the first artist I hired, I decided to find the artist that fit the book. Chanel loves books and her art spoke to me and let me know that she was the right artist to create the cover for *Hold Space*. Later, she confessed that creating a book cover was a dream of hers, so this is a debut for both of us! Keep an eye on her, because she's doing big things.

I went through several rounds of edits on my own and realized sections that needed to be added and hired the perfect editor, Deborah Sosin. She challenged me and gave me positive feedback and excellent constructive criticism. It was exactly what I and the book needed! And Robert Burke Warren, the creative Jack-of-all-Trades, (writer and editor by day, musician by night) did my final edit and I'm grateful his eyes and "red pen" were on it.

I cannot forget to thank our handsome polydactyl cat, who sat with me while I typed away, sometimes forcing his way on my lap to take a moment to just be. And our sweet little Muppet-dog for making sure I took breaks to take her outside or share my breakfast.

To all my spirit guides and guardian angels who supported my writing before they passed or always from the other side. They cheered me on or whispered "Write!" in my ear over and over until I got back to it. To those on the other side who read my early writing and cheered me on, Aunt Cathy, Uncle Kevin, Marcelino Vasquez, and Elaine Witman, thank you for being my team on the other side. I heard and felt Aunt Cathy many times while writing this book. To my maternal Grandpa, thanks for the many hints you dropped about Heaven while you were here.

Last, but not least, I thank all my teachers, especially Mokshapriya Shakti and Anita D'Onofrio, friends, extended family, students (yoga and reiki), and clients through the years. Each and every one of you had an impact on who I am today and the energy and sentiment of this book.

INTRODUCTION

Congratulations and welcome to your life! The journey into awakening happens now, as we drop the ego or logic brain and tap into our creative/intuitive brain and trust our soul's blueprint to lead us to peace, health, and authenticity.

Hold Space is intended to be part of your self-care toolkit. It includes inspiring thoughts and affirmations addressing life's most difficult and challenging moments. The affirmations are not just happy words. They are also an acknowledgment of what's keeping you from being happy, and a poetic redirection to your true self. This book is like a roadmap back to you. Underneath all the emotional baggage, anger, trauma, anxiety and anything else keeping us from enjoying life, there is the true essence of each of us. By holding a space in time and energy, we create a safe environment to find that true self, heal the hurts, let go of the pain, and begin loving ourselves. Accept and embrace all that you are and live your truth, unapologetically!

Healing is not about changing who you are, but instead a process of dropping the act you've been performing for too many years. Negative thoughts are junk food for our inner critic. Those thoughts manifest what we *don't* want. Let's clear the mind of clutter that doesn't serve a good or healthy purpose. Goodbye fear, worries, limiting beliefs, shame, and doubt! Let's make room to hold space for faith, trust, and love.

When we are not living our life authentically, when we are following old patterns that lead nowhere but a pity party or resentment, we have to change course. When we get sick, we care for ourselves until we are well. When we give our power to other people, we have to go through all the feelings of unworthiness, shame and fear causing us pain or illness in our souls, and replace that with love. Only then are we able to start building our health back up at the foundation of our purest self. Keep listening. Keep breathing. You can start this book in any chapter or wherever resonates most now and begin the healing. Keep reading and moving forward. You can heal the old wounds that have been festering and begin loving yourself.

Healing is neither pretty nor easy, and I know this from my own experiences of many life challenges and trauma. I have written this book from my authentic self, my truth, and my heart. There is so much of my own healing journey and the awakening journeys of many clients that is relevant to each and every one of us. We are each a work in progress and that is what makes life more colorful. The human experience is filled with pain, fear, anger, sadness, and all other colors of emotions. It is a beautiful vision to watch someone step into their own truth, their confident, unapologetic self and just be.

The affirmations in this book will also help you feel more in harmony and balance with yourself; in addition, you will find a few exercises to help you work some stuff out. There are also a handful of meditations. All of the tools in this book help you connect to your subconscious mind and create new pathways in the brain to help you break the painful or negative cycles and patterns that you follow out of comfort. If you're reading this book, those pathways you've been following have not been serving your highest good! Here's the perfect time to try something new!

As you work through *Hold Space*, you can go in order or skip around. Some topics are easier than others and everyone must do each chapter in their own time. Every one of us is a masterpiece in progress and it takes time to see what the world (the part that hasn't been keeping you down) sees. Michelle's intention is for every reader to live life without any regrets or remorse. Wherever you are, whatever age you may be, there is something in this book that will help you show yourself some compassion and heal.

When doing the meditations in this book, find a comfortable place to sit or lay down without distractions. It's best to close your eyes, even if it's just in between breathing. Each meditation is simple enough that you can read it and then close your eyes and visualize, stay with it, then go back and read the next section. If you feel like you keep falling out of the meditation by glancing back at the book, audio files of the guided meditations can be downloaded at MyReikiHealer.com.

I am not a licensed psychologist, medical doctor, or healthcare professional and this book provides no guarantees and does not replace the care of doctors or other healthcare professionals. This book is based on my personal experiences, my own work in therapy, trainings I've participated in, and from my 13 years of experience as a Reiki Master, Akashic Records reader, spiritual channel, and yoga teacher. I wish you healing and hope that you start loving yourself soon.

IF YOU ARE IN CRISIS, CALL:

> **The National Sexual Assault Hotline:** 1-800-656-4673 or **The Suicide Prevention Hotline:** 1-800-273-TALK (8255). If you can't bear to speak about it, but prefer to chat online, RAINN (**rainn.org**) has that option!
> And **The Trevor Project/Trevor Lifeline** has three options: 1-866-7386. There is also a chat option and you can reach out by text by texting "Start" to 678-678.
> There is help and understanding out there.

Chapter 1

The Soul

"Whatever you are physically...male or female, strong or weak, ill or healthy--all those things matter less than what your heart contains. If you have the soul of a warrior, you are a warrior. All those other things, they are the glass that contains the lamp, but you are the light inside."
– Cassandra Clare, *Clockwork Angel*

I AM

I AM = Divinity
For many I AM = God
For those that prefer a more earth-based higher power,
I AM = Purity or the Universe

"I AM" is the start of many affirmations as a recognition of the divine light we each have.

In Buddhism, Hinduism, Judaism, and other religions, there is a phrase that means "I am who I am" or "I am that I am." In each of these religions, spiritual groups, new age groups, and within the Reiki circles, I AM represents the divine or holy source. By saying "I am that I am" or "I am who I am," we are saying "I am one with the divine." Within each of us is a divine light, our soul essence that is our life force energy, our prana, or our chi. Without source, there is no "I AM." Each of us is part of source, and together we are all connected as source. There is really no "I," but "we," and once we find balance with our own individual souls, we can join with one another as a collective—one love, one humanity, all one.

I Am Open

I am in total harmony.
I am at peace.
I have hope.
I have faith in humanity and the heavens.
I am awakening.
I am a student of the universe and of the earth.
I humbly learn all the lessons that I must to evolve and
become enlightened.
I have faith in my own divinity, the light of my soul.
I have faith in Source.
I AM Source.
I am connected to all that is.
I am all that is.
I AM!

"I am that I am" also means "I am here below" (in a body on the earth) and "I am above" (in Heaven/higher self).

As without, so within.
As above, so below.
So it is.

Many energy workers or light workers use this expression. As the soul awakens, we realize we are expressions of the universe, and the universe is experiencing itself through each of us. It is like a diamond with its many facets that reflect and refract light. The diamond looks different from every angle. Just as the earth or the universe looks different for each of us. And it may appear different depending on what we're going through at that moment. If we're sad and lonely, the world and universe seems cold. When we're happy, every bird is singing for us!

As without, so within:
>
> All that is in the universe is within each and every one of us. We have access to all the wisdom of the universe inside us. Every answer we need can be found deep within. It can be found through prayer, meditation, yoga, tai chi, qi gong, or any form of stillness or mindful movement.

As above, so below:
>
> All that is within the universe, the heavens, or the multiverse is also reflected here on earth. Souls choose to come here to grow, to play, to evolve in whatever way they need or want. In the physical world, we have much more emotional range. The biggest difference here is that we have anger, fear, and ego. Heaven has omniscience; we know everything from every life there. We have the power to access some of that here, just as our souls can experience all the colors and shades of light and dark in this lifetime.

So it is.

The Namaste Effect

In Yoga, we say "Namaste." Same say it is a greeting, but it is more like "aloha" or "shalom." It is both a greeting, a validation and a goodbye. Namaste has many translations that basically mean the same thing, but the nuance that resonates with me and how I always describe it to my students is, "The divine light in me, recognizes the divine light in you." It is very much like the feature film, *Avatar* with the phrase, "I see you."

Underneath our skin, muscles, organs, bones, we are all souls, connected by energy. Every single person we see, bump into, befriend or marry has shared energy with us. No matter what is going on with that person, we can shift the narrative if we find a place of compassion and say "Namaste." I call this, The Namaste Effect.

When we can pause, take a few breaths, and find the purest part of ourselves and find the purest part of another person, we find peace. The Namaste Effect is not easy to master, but the more we practice, the better we get. When we find ourselves judging someone we don't know: Namaste. When we are fighting with family: Namaste. When we are holding onto guilt: Namaste from our higher, spirit self to our earthly self. Namaste helps us hold space for compassion, peace, love, and healing.

Connection to All

*I have access to all the knowledge and wisdom of the earth
and the universe within my body, mind, and soul.
With that knowledge and wisdom,
I can heal my body, mind, and soul.
I heal with love.
I heal with trust.
I heal with faith.
I am safe in my body.
I am safe in my mind.
I am safe in my soul.
I am connected to all that is on this earth
and in the universe.
May these connections help balance
my body, mind, and soul.
May I rise to my highest vibration possible today.
May I heal all that is ready to heal in this moment.
All is in divine order.
I am perfectly me.
Hell yes, I AM!*

Nature Healing

The moon, the sun, the stars, the wind, the rain, and the earth. We are all here to share and enjoy it. Nature is part of us and we are part of nature. Those days when you feel like you're spinning out of control or circling the drain into depression, look to nature. Look up to the sky. There is psychological evidence that looking up and looking to the sky, a sunset, a sunrise, the clouds, the moon, or the stars are ways to get grounded and rebalance. The rebalance of energy works with our subconscious brain and reminds us that we are part of something bigger than ourselves. Sometimes even consciously realizing that the moon or sun will rise again tomorrow is enough for us to carry on.

Our mind's eye has a specialized interpretation of things we see in our lower field of vision as well as the field of vision above the horizon. Neuroscientist Fred Previc, author of *The Dopaminergic Mind in Human Evolution and History,* argues that the visual system that specializes in the area above the horizon is highly developed in human beings. This processing area of the brain is lit up during meditation, reiki, dreaming, daydreaming, religious experiences, and likely most creative and imaginative activities that help us to expand beyond ourselves and the limitations of space and time. When we realize there is more to life than this crappy moment, this grief, this pain, or whatever it is we are going through, it can help restore peace and balance within the body-mind-soul temple.

Nature, in particular, is a free and effective quick fix for those moments when life feels overwhelming. Of course, if you are feeling completely hopeless and considering hurting yourself, then please call 800-273-8255. You matter! You are needed! I promise that you are here for a purpose. Hang on and FIGHT for your life! Survive now and thrive later.

Look to the Sky

When you feel
lost...
helpless...
hopeless...
unseen and unheard,
Look up to the sky
the moon...
the stars...
and the clouds...
These constants remind us that we can carry on
One day...
One hour...
One minute at a time.

Free Will

Each of us is born with free will. Even if we are born or live in a country that doesn't allow much freedom, there is still free will of the individual. In different societies, some freedom may be removed or withheld; but in the spiritual sense, we each have free will. We choose when to go to bed at night. We choose what we eat, drink, or whom we love.

We are born perfect. In fact, before we are born, we choose our parents out of all the potential souls in the world. We even select both the egg and the sperm that we want to merge to create the physical form that we are meant to be to help us become an even better version of ourselves.

Every choice that we make in life is an exercise of free will. From the day of birth, we cry to let others know what we need. Once we can crawl, we go after what we want. Once we can speak, we tell others what we want and need.

Free will doesn't mean that we take what we want or do harm to others. Along with free will, we each have an inner compass of what is inherently good and "right"; we are born with unconditional love and divine light. There are morals, ethics, and parent-modeled guidelines in place for us, in society, and our families, to learn how the world works and how to live within the parameters of society. This does not have to dampen our will, our dreams, or our burning desires in life.

Every one of us is born with a soul blueprint, perfectly unique. Think of it as an outline of who we are and a map of what we intend to do in this lifetime. This map has multiple potential pathways to get to where we want to end up. With free will, we have the ability to take the long way through rocky roads, up tall mountains, or deep into ditches and caves. It's our choice.

We each have a spirit guide that has been mutually chosen (free will), that will be with us from the moment that we decided to be born until the day that we die (and sometimes beyond that). This guide will often help us stay on course or guide us back to people, places, or situations we must face in order to move forward.

Sometimes we feel like we're spinning our wheels or covering the same ground with the same relationships or bosses, while our spirit guide is trying to guide us to consider other choices, actions, or reactions.

We are each born with a moral compass and free will, while our guides help us stick to it and our soul blueprint, which is stored in our energetic field, below the earth's surface. We have the opportunity to learn from every experience, positive or negative. It's our free will to perceive life experiences as positive or identify the hard lessons as fucked-up karma. There's no such thing. All choices bring us forward to self-discovery, whether we discover what we no longer like and want to change, or realize we are exactly where we need to be and in awe of how homey it feels. When we live in alignment with our blueprint, we are content. If life feels like challenge after challenge, it may be an opportunity to look at our life choices and maybe make some tweaks.

Just as there is free will in life, there is free will in this book to skip around and do the exercises, affirmations, or meditations you choose. It is our responsibility and decision to accept ourselves or not. There will be lots of opportunities to explore and reflect. If we keep an open mind during life's challenges and take a chance on ourselves, great rewards are usually ahead. Be brave. Be bold. Each of us is worthy of a good life. Say it out loud:

I am brave.
I am bold.
I am steady.
I am ready.

"If we could change ourselves, the tendencies in the world would also change. As a man changes his own nature, so does the attitude of the world change towards him... We need not wait to see what others do."
– Gandhi

Change

In energetic or spiritual work, there is no good or bad, right or wrong; everything just is. Trees don't loathe themselves as their leaves change color and they certainly don't cry when their leaves begin to fall. Snakes shed their skin and slither on. Caterpillars don't worry about creating a chrysalis out of their own bodies and transforming into a butterfly; they just do it! Change is good.

As human beings, we are likely the only species to reason and rationalize. Through rationalization, sometimes guided by fear, guilt, or feelings of unworthiness, we sometimes put ourselves last or choose less than what we really want or need so as to satisfy others' needs first. Or we choose or accept what we do not want out of fear. We talk ourselves out of changing or doing things to improve ourselves. Enough! We should not hold ourselves back out of fear or what we think is best for someone else. Unless it is our own child, it's a trap we set for ourselves, over and over again. We have to let people know that we matter and we have feelings, thoughts, and needs.

Let's create some damn boundaries! Even children need boundaries once they are old enough to reason a bit themselves. The perfect time to start modeling such boundaries is when children are in grade school, when they have to learn to wait their turn or ask for help. "Mommy needs alone time to take a shower," is one example of that. When we set boundaries, we create structure for our children and immediately let them know that they have rights and their own boundaries too. When a parent lives in truth, following dreams, working hard to achieve and enjoys doing it, the child recognizes that life can be hard, but each person has a right to follow their dream. Remember that, in the early years, parents are the only people children see every day. Yes, babysitters, nannies, teachers, and grandparents are often around, but parents are the primary models for what is right and good in the world.

The universe wants us to achieve our dreams and throws opportunities in front of us all the time. Sometimes, it takes big shifts to wake us up. When we lose that job that we hated, we don't have to look at it with fear. It's important to allow ourselves the time to grieve, mourn, and even freak out a little, but just a little, because it's actually an opportunity for us to discover something great about ourselves! Leaving a job where we felt unappreciated can open doors for a better future with a company that recognizes our talent and makes us excited to go to work every day!

No matter what changes happen in life, we will always be ourselves at the core. Events can spur us to create new facets of ourselves, even if they leave scars, but the essence of our selves and our souls remains profoundly perfect. We must trust and have faith. Say and believe it: "I got this!"

Embracing Change

I embrace change.
I trust in the process of transition and transformation.
I have faith that better opportunities and days are ahead.
I know that I am happy and fulfilled in the future.
Today, I begin taking steps to arrive at that happy time,
By choosing to accept each event with
an open heart and an open mind.
I am ready!

Chapter 2

Self-Care & Holding a Space for You

"Doesn't a hug deserve a hug too?!"
– Pops, The Regular Show

Keeping Busy vs. Me Time

I saw a meme that said, "Be so busy you have no time to be sad." That's setting you up for failure! Sadness and depression don't work that way. People can maintain day-to-day function and still be depressed. People grieve for years and are still sad while they work their asses off! A statement like that is encouraging us to compartmentalize or stuff our feelings down indefinitely. That is a recipe for an endless cycle of feeling like our feelings don't matter.

We can do things, even if we're sad or depressed or angry or grieving. Some tasks may require us to put feelings aside temporarily, like our jobs or our children. We can even enjoy the little moments in our lives while feeling another emotion at the same time. All of this is natural.

But we deserve time to ourselves to just be. We are worthy! Let's take time to **SIT WITH OUR FEELINGS**. Let's be present with why we feel this way and explore how we can do something to change it, like love ourselves a little more fully. It's okay to be sad sometimes. It's not against the law to be depressed. No matter where we are or what we are feeling, we are okay. I sometimes hug myself in times of sadness, darkness, or anger. Sometimes I wish someone would hug me when I feel unsafe or out of control. How about we hug ourselves when we need a hug?

Sit With Yourself Meditation

Close your eyes. Take a few deep, slow breaths. Allow yourself to fully relax every muscle in your body, your feet, legs, hands, shoulders, jaw, and face. Bring your attention to your mind's eye. In the darkness of your closed eyes, allow a picture of you as a child come into focus in your mind. Imagine your younger self is sitting across the room from you. How old is that younger version of you? What was going on for you at that age? Have a little chat with your younger self as if you are an adult in that time of your life. Show yourself the compassion you wish you had received then!

Imagine that you're hugging yourself then, or whenever it was that the world or people first let you down. You can invite your inner child of any age to this loving moment. Hold that space. Just be with yourself. Can you sit with the pain and emotions for just a few minutes? You can shout, *"Why?!"* and not worry about the answer. You are allowed to feel however and whatever emotion you feel until you start to feel better.

When that time comes, if you can, tell your younger self how much you love them. Remind yourself that you're okay, in the past, present, and even in the future. You're a survivor and you are growing into an awakened soul!

Bring your attention back to your breath. Wiggle your fingers and toes. Wrap your arms around yourself in real time. Do this as often as you like, especially when you are feeling unloved or unworthy. You are loved and you are worthy of that love.

Me Time

I release all thoughts, energy,
and feelings weighing me down.
I release all responsibility
for other people's emotions and baggage.
I am free from the chains of all that I cannot control.
I am free to live my own life
and have my own identity and autonomy.
I am empowered to speak my truth
and express my needs.
I am seen and heard!
I am enough.
I am worthy.
I matter.
I AM!

Holding a Space for Healing

Not long ago, my husband and I were at the drive-thru at Dunkin Donuts picking up an order he'd placed through the app. They asked his name and after he answered, they said, "We got you."

I immediately felt the power of that phrase. It felt so comforting: "We got you." Many times when my children were crying, I would hold them and say, "I got you. Mommy's got you." Even when my dog is startled by a noise, I'll hold her and say, "I got you." It's a powerful phrase of comfort.

As our daughter got words, she would hold up her arms and say, "I hold you," when she needed comforting or to be held. Again, powerful statement! She wanted to be held, but said it as "I hold you." She had heard "I got YOU" so many times that she knew exactly what she needed and mimicked the way she had heard it. There is great power in the phrase, just as there is great power in literally holding someone, hugging them, and just being with them. That is the power of holding a space for someone, holding a supporting space for a person in need. "I got you." Sit with these words for a few minutes. Repeat them out loud.

I got you.
We got you.
I hold you.

How many times do we feel unsupported or like no one has our back? We all feel like no one has us, sometimes. Women and mothers, in particular, often experience this. "Women's work," even today—the unpaid, invisible work and emotional information stored in women's brains—still goes unnoticed, underappreciated, and undervalued. Sorry guys, you may feel it too, but society definitely has set a precedent for this imbalance.

Whoever you are and no matter your gender, race, or background, how powerful is it when someone says, "I got you"? When we know someone has our back, sees us, and wants to support us, even if it's merely encouragement at Dunkin, that feeling goes a long way. It hits us deeply to know that someone is holding a space for our well-being.

Let's take a moment to hold a space for everyone we know who may be needing support right now. We must also hold a space for ourselves in this vision. People need people, but we absolutely need to be there for ourselves.

Hold Space

I hold space for:
Anyone who has lost a loved one.
Anyone struggling to become.
Anyone who is suffering in silence and selflessness.
Anyone who feels powerless.
The anxious and depressed.
For all those who are awakened and see the truth
but aren't sure what to do next.
Anyone living in fear.
Anyone lost.
Anyone who feels unloved.
All who are healing.
All who are awakening.
Any who are starting on their path to greatness!
I got you.

Creating Boundaries

Holding a space for ourselves and our well-being lets others know what lines not to cross. You might have heard the proverb: "Do not drink poison to quench a thirst." This proverb is the perfect example of why we need boundaries:

We can't heal in the place where we were poisoned when the poison is still being served.

This is not an easy one. For many reading this book, home was or is a toxic or dysfunctional environment. Sometimes, we don't realize how toxic the environment is until we leave. It's like carbon monoxide poisoning. Carbon monoxide is a silent killer; it has no scent, taste, or warning, unless you have a working detector. If you inhale enough of it, it causes drowsiness and confusion. We don't realize we are being poisoned. We slowly go to sleep and might not wake up.

It is similar in relationships sometimes. We can acknowledge and possibly even keep relationships with people who no longer serve our highest good, but only if we create boundaries. This is not easy. Boundaries are hardest to enforce with people who respect them the least. When a person has an expectation of who you are to them and refuses to see it any other way, it might be in your best interest to let them go if setting boundaries doesn't work.

Boundaries are like holding a space for ourselves and our well-being while letting others know what lines not to cross. When we were children and someone pulled our hair, the teacher might state our boundaries or boundaries for the class (and society): "Now Charles, we do not pull people's hair. It's not nice." That is what is needed for us to succeed and thrive. Even as adults, we sometimes have to revisit our boundaries and edit them or reinforce old ones we have allowed to be breached. When we spend a little time considering what we need or what our triggers are, we can set boundaries that help us thrive. For example:

"Your sarcasm makes me feel like you enjoy hurting my feelings. Please be direct with me if you have a problem. I don't find sarcasm funny."

Boundaries can be related to time, touch, or topics. For example, we may have a relative we can only be around or speak with for under 15 minutes before they make us feel unsafe and triggered. We absolutely need boundaries for energy vampires! Certain kinds of touch can be triggering and off limits for some, but okay with our safest, closest people. We each get to decide our boundaries. Boundaries hold a space for us to feel safe to enjoy life and be vulnerable without fear. What does that look like? We can ask our families to avoid any topics that we don't want to discuss, such as politics, religion, or sexuality. We can create a safe word with our closest friends and family for them to know when we are triggered and need them to stop talking, yelling, or touching us. We can offer an alternative instead: "If you feel like you need to bring up politics, warn me so I can leave the room."

When we are triggered, we need to hold a space for ourselves and learn what we need most in that moment to survive. Later, we need to hold a space for ourselves to sit with the feelings and have an internal conversation about the present moment and feel steady and grounded and invulnerable to the hurt or trauma of the past.

Explore the who, what, where, when, why and how that you connect with the phrase "I am safe". We need to feel safe with ourselves, but **who** else do we feel safe with, without feeling indebted or burdensome? That can be anyone we share an unconditional love with, platonic or romantic. **What** activities or topics of conversations make you feel safe and grounded? **Where** in the world do we feel safe? When we're triggered, sometimes we don't even feel safe in our own bodies. Is there a place in the world that feels safe? It could be wrapped in a blanket or a comfy chair or at the beach. Know what that is, so that you can visualize it whenever you need to feel safe. **When** do we feel the safest? **Why**? The **How** will be answered, naturally, once we know the answers to all the other questions. We must find out what we need to feel safe enough to be ourselves or just exist in the presence of others. Everyone's boundaries are different. To best set the boundaries that work for you, take time to explore your feelings and triggers, identify the challenging people and situations, then learn to set them with confidence and self-love.

I Am Protected
by a Shield of Divine Light

As I breathe deeply into my body,
I am reminded that I am safe.
As I breathe out,
I extend my energetic roots deep down into the earth;
I am steady.
I breathe in and feel a protective shield rising up from the
earth and surrounding me like a bubble of light.
As above, so below, this energetic field of protection
keeps me safe.
I am safe and protected from harm.
I am balanced and centered in this moment.
I am not alone.
I am empowered and unconditionally loved
by my guides, guardians, and angels.
I am healthy and balanced.
I am calm.
All is as it should be.
All is in divine order.

You Are NOT Your Brother's, Mother's, Father's, Sister's or Spouse's Keeper!

Often, the people we need to set the most boundaries with are in our family. Family members sometimes believe that we are the same person we were as a child and that the family dynamics never change. Not anymore! We are getting healthy. We are putting ourselves first now.

We can't be steady, grounded, or balanced if we're carrying other people's baggage, thoughts, programming, or feelings. We each must find our own balance to let that shit go! It wasn't ours in the first place. We cannot go through life responsible for other people, unless it is a child, and even then, there are limitations and boundaries that need to be set as they get older.

Be you! Speak your authentic truth. Express yourself and your truth through action, if not words. Live life as you see fit. No one else is on your life path, except for you. We do our best with what we know now. We all make mistakes along the way and will do better when we know better. Those mistakes are opportunities for learning. Every successful business owner is proud of the failures that led to success. Each living thing on this earth has to fight in life. When we make a mistake, we must get up, assess, go forward and get stronger. If we don't let babies fall down when they try to walk, they will never gain the strength to walk by themselves! Butterflies will not fly if they don't fight their way out of the chrysalis. Set your boundaries and value yourself. You are enough! Enjoy the journey.

I Release All That is Not Mine

I release all self-doubt.
I release all energy and feelings of less than.
I release all thoughts, energy, and feelings
weighing me down.
I release all responsibility for other people's emotions.
I send it back to the earth, the ocean, and the cosmos to be
neutralized into nothingness.
I am free from the chains of all I cannot control.
I am free to live my own life and speak my truth.
I am seen and heard.
I am strong.
I am balanced.
I am enough!
I am loved.
I am love.
I AM!

Protection: Aura

The aura is an energetic force field within and around our bodies. We are spiritual and energetic beings having a physical experience. Energy is the life force that each living thing on earth holds within them. Some call it chi, qi. or pranayama. Reiki is translated as universal life force energy, meaning that this energy resides all over the universe. Reiki is the practice of revitalization of that energy in the spiritual and physical aspects of a being. The aura is just one layer of our energy field, but a very important one, nonetheless.

When we're depleted or at a lower vibration, sad, run down, or fearful, we are more vulnerable because our energetic field is not strong enough to withstand negativity or dark energy. It's also a "like attracts like" scientific law of attraction. If we're feeling angry, we'll attract angry energy to reinforce that feeling or energetic value. When we're happy, feel valued, or at peace, we will attract that. And even if some negativity sneaks in, we will not accept the negativity as our truth; thus, we have the potential to turn someone else's mood around, too, because of the strength of our positive energetic field or aura.

When we resonate at a higher or optimal vibration, our aura is bigger and our energetic protective shield or barrier is stronger, like a force field around a spaceship in a sci-fi movie. When we are happy or in love, our aura is big and bright; even unhappy people might turn their frowns upside-down. The aura is stronger because the divine light within us is brighter and shining our truth. This is the real you! At peace, in love, and content is how life looks in the spirit world.

When we are in fear, our aura doesn't grow bigger to protect us; it actually retreats and gets smaller. It becomes a cycle, where become more fearful, because we feel more vulnerable without our protective layers. In this state, we are more vulnerable to other people's bad moods or negativity. Some people will even gain physical weight as an emotional response to serve as a layer of protection when they are in fear, PTSD or fight/flight/freeze mode.

It's important to keep our energetic or auric field intact and strong, especially when we feel depleted or in a weakened state. Even if we're sad or fearful, we have the power within to expand and reinforce our auric field with love. When we're mad at someone, we can still love them. That is, in essence, what we need to do when we are upset, angry, or afraid. We have to surround ourselves with unconditional self-love.

A lot of people working in the field of energy work or alternative medicine talk about white light. White light is, as we know from middle school science class, all colors of the light spectrum. Therefore, white light holds the frequencies of all the colors of the rainbow. In energy work all colors of the rainbow vibrate at a different frequency and align with the corresponding chakras of the matching color. There are a few exceptions, but that is the short of it.

As directed by my own early teachers, for many years, I'd call on white light protection or see myself in a white light bubble for protection. I cannot recall any specific time that it impacted me as much as when I chose to, instead, work with the pink light frequency of unconditional love in this bubble of light exercise. It was late one night, at the end of the week, on the subway coming home from Manhattan toward Brooklyn. I was tired and depleted and feeling a little too vulnerable to be on a crowded subway train, but then three people sitting around me started talking trash about people at work. All of them worked together. One was right next to me and the other two were in an L-shaped arrangement next to her. The car was full so I couldn't change seats. I could feel their negative energy pushing me to feel angry.

I closed my eyes and tuned in to my yoga training, ujjayi breath. This breath is very cleansing as the muscles in the back of the throat flex to make noise, like the sound of ocean waves. I chose this specific noisy breath to drown out the smack-talk and focus on the deep, oxygenating inhale and exhale through the nose, while I visualized pink light coming down from the heavens into my heart. I breathed into my lungs and heart chakra as I envisioned this pink light swirling around and growing bigger, filling my body, growing bigger and pushing past the physical body into a bubble or orb around me and I felt a release in my body into relaxation and peace.

Beyond my own breath, I noticed that the people, suddenly, had shifted their conversation to office birthdays and whose birthday was coming up next and what kind of cake they would have, blah, blah, blah…. I smiled before I opened my eyes. That pink light of unconditional love had gotten so big that it had hit them and they didn't even know it! **That** is a powerful boundary! There was no magic to this exercise and no overpowering the will of another person. In order for anyone to be affected by this light and loving energy, they have to be open to it. We are all energetic beings and everything on this planet is ruled by free will. I was thrilled with this result and, at that moment, I realized how powerful the pink light rays and unconditional love energy is.

Meditation on Love (Bubble of Light)

Begin each meditation by finding yourself a quiet place to sit or lay down comfortably for a short time. Your first attempt at meditation may take a little time, but breath is vital to getting yourself into a relaxed state of mind. For this meditation, ujjayi breath is best, but slowly and deeply is fine. If you are not familiar with ujjayi breath, it is the primary breathing technique we use in yoga practice. First, try to make the sound that you would make while fogging up a mirror. Ujjayi is very similar in the muscles we use to make the noise, but it is done with the mouth closed and both inhale and exhale are through the nose. It can sound similar to Darth Vader or if you get into a slow flow with the noise of the breath, it sounds a lot like ocean waves. Some even refer to it as ocean breath. Practice that breath nice and easy, inhale deeply and exhale slowly. Inhale deeply and exhale slowly. This helps you relax.

Shake out any parts of your body holding tension. Breathing in and gently shaking as you exhale. Relax the muscles in your jaw, your face, your neck and shoulders. Gently roll your neck or shoulders if they are tense. Bring your attention back to your breath.

I breathe in … visualizing a beautiful pink, fuzzy, soft glowing light of unconditional love coming down from the heavens, through the top of my head into my heart. I breathe out worry and fear.

I breathe in… The pink light swirling around inside my heart. I am calming down. I am safe and grounded in my body. The pink light swirls and spirals open inside my body… I breathe out doubt and sadness.

I breathe in… My body is calm. My mind is calm. My emotions are calm. I breathe out, the pink light filling up my entire body and glowing past the edges of my skin. I feel love. I feel loved. I am love.

I breathe in… The pink light is shaping into an orb or bubble of light around me. I am protected by a shield of unconditional love. I breathe out anything that does not serve me.

I breathe in… I am healthy and balanced. I am steady and

strong. I am safe. I am smiling! I am love. I breathe out and choose to share and spread love and smiles.

I am all that I am.

Chapter 3

Trust & Faith

"Nothing which is true or beautiful or good makes complete sense in any immediate context of history; therefore, we must be saved by faith."
– Reinhold Niebuhr

Trust & Faith

People often ask how we know things or how we are able to do certain things. We forget how spectacular we are, because our gifts are just there for us. Sometimes, effortlessly, we allow creativity to flow out of us or our intuition guides us, flawlessly, because we have trust and faith.

There is no instruction booklet on trust and faith. Believe me, I have struggled with it, particularly trust. With my own PTSD, I still have trust issues pop up from time to time. However, when it comes to trusting my gifts, divine guidance and "the clairs," ("The Clairs" is my nickname for clairvoyance, clairaudience, claircognizance, clairgustance, clairsentience and clairalience are all defined in chapter 11 in detail.) I'm in, 100 percent. If I'm unsure of something I saw, heard, or received, I'll wait for confirmation on the details, but I trust in the transmissions.

It's a very individual and personal path for each of us to trust in ourselves and find faith in the divine. And I say that to anyone, even an atheist, because we have to have faith in something! Even if it's our own moral compass, we have something guiding or driving us in life.

Grounded to the Earth,
Connected to the Heavens

I am grounded to the earth.
I am safe and steady.
I am connected to the heavens.
I am protected.
I have access to all the wisdom and knowledge
of the earth and the universe
Without and within my body, mind, and soul.
I have all the courage, confidence, compassion,
and clarity I need
to move forward on my life journey.
I trust in myself.
I have faith in me and the power of positive energy
in the universe.
As above, so below, so it is.

Surrender:
Can You Let Go & Have Faith?

Many of us have secret or silent burdens we carry with us day to day. Sometimes we know about them, but they are wrapped in shame, so we don't unburden ourselves to anyone about them. We just keep carrying them. Some of us are born worriers, the deep thinkers of the tribe who consider all the options and calculate risks. Even if we're neither, we all have moments of being weighed down by our worries, responsibilities, or our past pain or trauma.

If there are emotional and mental burdens that we cannot handle or that we do not have the power to change, we are meant to have faith that they will work out the best way and for the greater good of as many as possible. We can also meditate, pray or call on our guardian angels or spirit guides for guidance or assistance.

When I'm working with clients in Reiki sessions, I often find a common thread linking the healing work of all the clients throughout a week. When this happens, that theme is often something universal that my spirit guides want me to share with many. This is another aspect of how this book came to be. A while back a message I channeled from each of their spirit guides and guardian angels was: "Lay your burdens down." Simple enough, right? Why do we forget to do this?

With one client, the spirit guides presented this concept with the song "Jesus, Take the Wheel" by Carrie Underwood. A while back, there was a Vine (a video app like TikTok, but all videos were eight-seconds or less) of a person driving who lifts his hands off the steering wheel and a man dressed like Jesus leans in through the car window and takes the steering wheel. It was a silly video (you can find it on YouTube: Jesus take the wheel vine) and as this song popped into my head, so did this funny visual during a very serious session, but that's the point: Sometimes, we take ourselves and life too seriously. We have the power to make great changes in ourselves and in humanity, but there are some things that we are not equipped, nor able to change, fix, or handle. Let them go.

This is very much like the serenity prayer, which many people in 12-step recovery programs use. The message offers a great way to live, whether you are in recovery or not. The simple one we know is easy to remember and carry around with us. It's three lines!

"God, grant me the serenity to accept the things I cannot change, the courage to change the things I can, and the wisdom to know the difference."
– Reinhold Niebuhr

However, when we read the full prayer, by Reinhold Niebuhr, it is a masterpiece of the "Lay your burdens down," "Give it up to God," or "Jesus, take the wheel!"

Religion can absolutely be removed from the meaning of the serenity prayer. Instead of "God" or "Jesus," choose "Mother Nature," your higher self, angels or even a loved one who has passed on. We can have faith without following a particular religion. We don't have to go to church or temple to believe in God, Jesus, Buddha, or any other ascended soul. We can certainly have faith in the universe that there is more out there than we know or can understand in our conscious brains. We know that vibrations can affect others in close proximity as well as far away. We know our words of anger or fear can harm someone without laying a hand on their physical body.

Prayer for Serenity

"God, grant me the serenity
to accept the things I cannot change,
the courage to change the things I can,
and the wisdom to know the difference.
Living one day at a time,
enjoying one moment at a time;
accepting hardship as a pathway to peace;
taking, as Jesus did,
this sinful world as it is,
not as I would have it;
trusting that You will make all things right
if I surrender to Your will;
so that I may be reasonably happy in this life
and supremely happy with You forever in the next.
Amen."

— Reinhold Niebuhr

You don't have to believe any particular aspect of religion, but do have faith that there's more to learn and that none of us knows everything. This will help us find peace and unburden ourselves of the emotional, mental, and spiritual weight we carry.

I sometimes wonder if Niebuhr actually practiced Reiki, because the ethical principles of Usui Reiki have some similar values. Here's my little play on the serenity prayer, mixed with Reiki principles:

Just for today,
I will not stress over the things I cannot control.
I will be brave and face the things I can.
I will breathe and remain calm through all of it!

Faith and trust are the virtues that help us arrive at inner peace. But inner peace is not to be confused with nirvana.

Nirvana, or *moksha,* is a transcendent state in which there is neither suffering, desire, nor sense of self, and the subject is released from the effects of karma and the cycle of death and rebirth. It represents the final goal of Buddhism. It is perfect, flawless happiness. That, usually, can be achieved only in death. However, contentment is the balance that we can achieve in life—the feeling of peace that is perfectly balanced in the center of all other emotions and feelings. There's no extreme anger, fear, grief, or even ecstatic passion or happiness. Contentment is the closest level of peace and joy that we can achieve and **maintain** on earth, in a body and a world with so much depth and layers of feelings and conflict.

Some of the most faithful on earth believe that we can achieve a higher level of peace as we work together to raise the vibration of the earth as a planet and humanity as a people. All one, like Bob Marley, John Lennon, and so many other songwriters felt, wrote, and sang. That level of peace is possible, but it cannot be done by one person alone. It starts with one person getting their act together and having faith and seeking peace. Then they start attracting others who are also seeking that level of peace. When people believe so strongly and have such incredible faith, they attract more and more people of peace and faith mindset, and all soon have the power to manifest the fuck out of their lives in peace, unity, and unconditional love.

Love, Trust, & Faith

I have access to all the knowledge and wisdom
Of my body,
The earth
And the universe.
With that knowledge and wisdom
I can heal my body, mind, and soul.
I heal with love.
I heal with trust.
I heal with faith.
I love, trust, and have faith in myself, the universe, and all
living beings on this earth.
I am safe in my body.
I am safe in my mind.
I am safe in my soul.
I am bathed in love, trust, and faith.
I am cleansed and purified in love, trust, and faith.
I am healed in love, trust, and faith.

Dorothy's Journey Back to Herself
(Heart, Brain, Courage, Home)

Every character in *The Wizard of Oz* already possessed all that they were searching for on their journey, a heart, a brain, courage and home, yet they persisted without realizing their truth. We have all the answers within us. The wisdom of all that we are is available to us through our high heart chakra (more about this on page 188). We have resources of wisdom as we need them. Until then, a space is being held for our highest wisdom, our highest frequency, and our greatest good. The key is to value ourselves and have confidence and faith that we are whole and the answers are always within. When we are quiet and journey deep inside, past the doubt, fear, the inner critic, and limiting beliefs, we will find the answers. To do that, as we've seen, we must have **trust** and **faith.**

In the movie, Dorothy feels unappreciated and invisible in her little black-and-white world. As far as she's concerned, the only one who sees her is her dog, Toto. And that bitch on the bicycle sees Toto as a menace and is ready to put him to death. Dorothy isn't heard when she's afraid someone wants to kill her only friend. Everything in the beginning is black and white in her eyes, because she is young and can't see that the adults are preparing for a bigger disaster, the storm.

All the same people in her life are present in Oz, though in different forms. All those people she thinks didn't care are there with her on her technicolor journey back to herself, her home! There, as a team, they value her. They protect her. She feels safe. She feels seen and supported. She feels loved.

We have helpers around us all the time. We choose many of the people in our lives to be there at specific times, and the duration of their presence in our lives does not devalue what they mean to us. They each help us rediscover ourselves. They may challenge us, our fears, our limiting beliefs so that we can rise above them and find truth. Sometimes, they help open our eyes to see the potential that we could not visualize beyond the illusion we were stuck in.

The group that travels along the yellow brick road together takes care of one another. There are no secrets. Each of them feels safe in their vulnerability. There is trust, an unspoken "This is my weakness, please keep me safe."

Each of the characters on the journey to Oz are presented to us as misfits who we wouldn't necessarily put together in a group, but they do fit. They protect one another, knowing their weaknesses, without criticism, but instead, with compassion. There is an unspoken "I got you" from each of them to the other. They put any differences aside and find their greatest level of strength and confidence within, especially when defending themselves as individuals or as a group. That is the subconscious heart brain taking over the body! Love is greater than any fear. This is their chosen family—the tribe they need to complete the journey and the challenges they must overcome along the way.

It's always easier to see how far you've come when looking back, rather than the progress you've made while you're progressing. The characters already have what they need and what they think they were lacking. Through the mirroring they provide one another, they are able to allow that truth into the light and be what they thought they weren't: The Scarecrow had a brain with both analytical and intuitive capabilities all along their journey; the Tin Man had heart every step of the way, expressing brotherly care for Dorothy and the rest of the group; the Lion had courage and stood up to anyone who threatened them; and Dorothy had the power to return home all along, because she had really never left: She was asleep in bed, at home, dreaming. Each of them was complete and whole, but a little more self-aware by the end.

Finding our tribe in adulthood is essential. This is not necessarily the family we were born into, because our family members may have fulfilled their purpose already. It's okay and expected to let them go to an extent (or fully) because of that. As adults, we find our kindred spirits to help us along life's path. These are the people we trust to help us rediscover the beauty of our imperfections, leveling up as we find our very own true voice. These are the souls who can say honestly and wholeheartedly, "I got you," and mean it as we journey to find truth.

Having confidence in our own voice, our truth, is vital! Speak up!

Step into the Light

I stand steady,
Feet firmly planted on the ground.
Gravity and all elements of nature and earth
are supporting me.
I exist and I am seen.
I have a voice and I am heard.
I march to the rhythm
of my own frequency and vibration.
I am perfectly me, for all to see.
I trust in the universe to continue to support me,
to help me attract others who are like me
or who can help me recognize my true self.
For my greatest good,
may my truth and the essence of my spirit shine.
May I empower others to shine brightly.
I am empowered!
I have free will.
I am in control of my own life.
I had the power all along.
I am ready to trust in myself,
to step forward on my path,
and march into the light,
May I skip along the path and enjoy the journey…
I shine light on the darkness I fear;
it is no longer scary.
I tap my feet to the earth with each step
on this life's path.
The destination?

(continued…)

I've already arrived.
I only have to open my eyes to recognize;
I'm already home.
As without, so within.
As above, so below.
So it is...
I'm home.
I AM.

Chapter 4

The Chakras: Safe & Grounded

"Our deepest fear is not that we are inadequate. Our deepest fear is that we are powerful beyond measure. It is our light, not our darkness that most frightens us. We ask ourselves, 'Who am I to be brilliant, gorgeous, talented, fabulous?' Actually, who are you not to be? You are a child of God. Your playing small does not serve the world. There is nothing enlightened about shrinking so that other people won't feel insecure around you. We are all meant to shine, as children do. We were born to make manifest the glory of God that is within us. It's not just in some of us; it's in everyone. And as we let our own light shine, we unconsciously give other people permission to do the same. As we are liberated from our own fear, our presence automatically liberates others."
– Marianne Williamson, *A Return to Love: Reflections on the Principles of A Course in Miracles*

The Chakras

Chakra is a Sanskrit word meaning "wheel," and each wheel is said to be a subtle or spiritual life force energy center within the body. Each chakra energy center or wheel keeps organs, glands, and areas of the body in balance. When in alignment and harmony, the entire body, mind, and soul unit is in good health, harmony, and peace. In order to align with our true selves, we must address the chakras and work to balance each of them.

The chakras are a subtle energy system that were discovered around 1500 to 500 BC in India. It was discussed in the Vedas, ancient religious texts that are said to be the word of God. Chakras are spinning disks or wheels of energy within the human body and beyond the body. The chakras are said to be directly connected to the health and well-being of the body, mind, emotions, and soul. Every chakra oversees a different area, gland, and organ within the body. The different chakras also coordinate with a different emotional-mental-physical health state or perspective. For now, we will focus on the seven primary chakras within the physical body. Repeat the following aloud:

I am the master of my body temple
I am safe in this body, space, and world.
I move through life with grace and confidence.
I am powerful beyond belief!
I can move mountains if I wish.

There is Strength in the Stillness, Waiting to Be Discovered

I breathe in:
I am steady and still.

I breathe out:
I let go of all doubt.

I breathe in:
I am safe.

I breathe out:
I release all fear.

I breathe in:
I am.

I breathe out:
I am that I am.

Root Chakra

All the chakras within the body match with a color on the visible light spectrum. The root chakra is the first one; it is located at the base of the spine and is said to resonate as the color red. It is called the Muladhara chakra in Sanskrit. In yogic traditions, the root chakra holds the energy of Kundalini and rises in a red spiral, like an uncoiling snake, up our spine, and helps us ground as well as embrace our passion and confidence.

The root or base chakra is the energetic home of our basic needs: shelter, food, safety, and security. Babies have very basic needs; they live in their root and crown chakras (discussed later in chapter 12). This chakra is activated at the moment of birth, when all babies are focused on: "Keep me alive, people!" This is where our survival instinct is felt and stored. As a baby, when our basic needs of safety and nurturing are fully met, we feel safe and grow up feeling generally supported by people and the constants in the world around us.

We may feel grounded to the earth, but if things are not optimal in a baby's life, they may feel that they are spiraling out of control with fear, anxiety, and a sense of threat. If a baby's survival needs are not met or trauma occurs in childhood, as adults, people may have deep fear and anxiety, or feel unsafe, ungrounded, and out of balance in the world or even in their own body. When one's childhood lacks a sense of autonomy and self-confidence, the world seems big and scary. Many of us have had this experience. So we have to go to the "root" of the problem—an imbalanced root chakra. We must clear that space and ground. Once we do, we feel more in harmony not only with the world around us, but also with ourselves.

In our spiritual aspect, there is a mirror image of all seven of the chakras in the body above, in the heavens, and below, in the earth. (As above, so below, so it is.) The fifth dimensional root chakra is the anchor point of our own ascended purpose and potential. This means that before we were born, all of our life goals and karmic baggage we wanted to address this time around is pre-programmed and guiding us forward on our life's journey in an intuitive, yet purposeful way. Yes, we have free will, but, as stated earlier, we have each chosen to be here at this particular time with our own soul blueprint, which holds all the subconscious information driving us to find our special purpose, learn lessons, and deal with past karma.

I Am Safe

I am safe in my body.
I am safe in my mind.
My soul is always protected and safe.
I am beautiful inside and out.
I am unconditionally loved and supported.
I am never alone.
I am valued.
I am loved.
I am.

Grounding

The word "grounding" is often overused, so much so that we've forgotten what it really means. The *Merriam-Webster Dictionary* defines "grounded" as "mentally and emotionally stable." To take that a step further into the energetic sense, grounded means that our energy is rooted to the earth, the realm, or planet where you live. Let's take it a step further and acknowledge gravity for a moment, as the force of nature that it is. By the force of gravity, we are held gently to the earth. With it, we find balance in our bodies. When we acknowledge and trust in gravity to support us and keep us steady, we are surrendering our imbalance back to the earth. We are in harmony with the force of gravity, the rotation of the earth, and the orbit around the sun. Even if we don't always feel supported or grounded, we are, indeed, part of humanity and connected to and supported by the energy around us.

When we are ungrounded, we feel out of sync with others. We feel out of balance physically, mentally, emotionally, or spiritually. We may feel unsafe in the world. We may even feel helpless and hopeless. This is textbook root chakra imbalance.

I Am Grounded

I breathe in.
I am grounded and steady.
Gravity and the earth hold me gently.
I breathe out.
I am connected to all living things on earth.
I breathe deeply in and connect to the seeds of
enlightenment within me.
I breathe out and breathe life into these seeds.
I breathe in the twinkling light of knowledge
growing inside me.
I breathe out doubt.
I breathe in and awaken the light within me.
I breathe out judgment of my dark and shadows.
I am in balance and harmony
with my light and dark.
I am filled with compassion and confidence.
I have access to all the wisdom of the earth
and the universe.
I am awakening.

Reconnecting to the True Self

Grounding is the physical connection between the electrical energetic frequencies of the human body with Earth's. When we practice grounding meditation, we are more present in ourselves. It is easier to focus on the present moment and feel more balanced and aware. Grounding ourselves and rooting to the earth's energy, we feel more calm, peaceful, and centered. The people, thoughts, and stimuli around us feel less stressful and threatening when we feel less like we're floating out in a threatening world and more like we are connected to and part of the earth itself.

In essence, grounding is reconnecting our spiritual self—the divine perfection of light that lives in each of us—with our bodies, to quiet our worried, busy, stressed-out minds.

Mountain Meditation

Find a comfortable place to sit or lie down. Sitting is preferred for a grounding meditation, because your root chakra is sitting on the earth. If you lie down, you can keep the knees bent and the feet on the floor so that you have that extra point of grounding. Or just find a comfortable resting position.

Feel your body touching the floor. Touch your palms to the chair, bed, floor, or mat below you. Take a deep breath in to the bottom of your lungs. Feel your rib cage expanding and your back touching closer to the floor.

Breathe in: *I am.* Breathe out: *Calm.*

Breathe in: *I am.* Breathe out: *Calm.*

Breathe in: *I am.* Breathe out: *Calm.*

Feel your body getting heavier on the floor. Feel your connection to the earth. Close your eyes for a moment and visualize light coming into your breath. Imagine yourself as part of the earth.

Breathe in: *I am a mountain.* Breathe out: *I am strong.*

Breathe in: *I am a mountain.* Breathe out: *I am supported.*

Breathe in: *I am a mountain.* Breathe out: *I am safe.*

See yourself as a mighty mountain. Feel the strength of your foundation. Feel the vast, wide base of your mountain. Imagine the many layers of bedrock below you. You are connected to the earth and all the layers below… the earth, the crust, the mantle, and the core.

If you have trouble visualizing or thoughts distract you, go back to your breath:

Breathe in: *I am a mountain.* Breathe out: *I am strong.*

Breathe in: *I am a mountain.* Breathe out: *I am supported.*

Breathe in: *I am a mountain.* Breathe out: *I am safe.*

Whether you are visual or not is not vital to this exercise. Feel your inner strength expanding through your body, your muscles, your mind, your nervous system. Relax.

Breathe in: *I am a mountain.* Breathe out: *I am strong.*

Breathe in: *I am a mountain.* Breathe out: *I am supported.*

Breathe in: *I am a mountain.* Breathe out: *I am safe.*
Feel the earth below you. Holding you gently.

Breathe in: *I am a mountain.* Breathe out: *I am supported.*

Feel the weight of your hands on the floor, on your belly, or in your lap. Imagine the warm sun beating down on you—this beautiful, mighty mountain.

Breathe in: *I am a mountain.* Breathe out: *I am safe.*
Keep breathing.

If emotions start to rise, keep breathing and acknowledge them. Imagine the excess emotions releasing through your exhale, tears, or energetically through the soles of your feet…into the earth below you. Let it go. Let it all go.

Send your breath and tension, negative thoughts, anger, grief, or fear deep into the earth. Let it go. Let it all go. Send it all through the layers of the earth, the crust, the mantle, and the core. At the core, see the red glowing orb of light. Feel its warmth. The earth's core is your anchor point. Feel gravity hugging you. Feel your connection to it.

Feel the reflected glow of the earth's core in your root chakra. Imagine its warm glow at the base of your spine, filling up the space of your lower back and pelvis.

Breathe in: *I am a mountain.* Breathe out: *I am strong.*

Breathe in: *I am a mountain.* Breathe out: *I am supported.*

Breathe in: *I am a mountain.* Breathe out: *I am safe.*

Imagine the red glow as an orb or a spiral of light around the base of your spine and tailbone. Imagine the glowing light splitting in two and running down your legs, out through the soles of your feet, into the earth, the crust, the mantle, until it finally meets the core. Send all that no longer serves you through this space. Let go of the emotional attachment to it as it leaves your body and releases out of your root chakra, down your legs, out through the soles of your feet, and deep down to the core of the earth. As you release all that no longer serves you…

Breathe in: *I am.* Breathe out: *Calm.*

Breathe in: *I am safe.* Breathe out: *I am calm.*

Feel the warmth of the fiery core cleansing the negative emotions, thoughts, and energy. Release all negativity to the fire. Clear all negativity, sending it into the fiery core. Bathe in the warmth of the healing fire. Cleanse in the warmth of the healing fire. Heal in the warmth of the sacred fire.

Breathe in: *I am safe.* Breathe out: *I am calm.*

Bring your attention back to your feet and root chakra. Imagine your mountain and at the top, a tree is beginning to grow. You are the tree, being birthed, renewed. Feel your roots growing deep down into the mountain and feel your leaves and trunk growing taller and taller, reaching for the sun. Fire below. Sun above. You are the tree of life. You are grounded to the earth, connected to the world and universe beyond. You are connected to all that is. You are all that you are. You are matter and **YOU MATTER.**

Now, imagine yourself sitting or lying under this tree of life. Like a tree, you are nurtured by the earth below and the sun and air above and around you. Feel the energy within you and around you. Feel the space around you and the body holding your spirit. Begin to feel your own body. Feel yourself grounded to the earth. To your body. Feel your energy, renewed, and refreshed.

Breathe in: *I am safe.* Breathe out: *I am calm.*

Breathe in: *I am safe.* Breathe out: *I am peaceful.*

Breathe in: *I am grounded.* Breathe out: *I am balanced.*

Breathe in: *I am grounded.* Breathe out: *I am balanced.*

Breathe in: *I am grounded.* Breathe out: *I am balanced.*

Breathe in and stretch your arms over your head and wiggle your toes down below. Feel the entire length and span of your body. Take a deep breath in and exhale with a sigh. Feel the space within your body and the space around you.

Breathe in: *I am grounded.* Breathe out: *I am balanced.*

If you are lying down, slowly roll to your side. Bring yourself to sitting. Inhale and reach your arms out to your sides.

Exhale and hug yourself. Hug with a new self-love. You are perfectly you. You are worthy of all the love and wisdom you seek. In your hug, pat your arms in an alternating rhythm. Tap your feet together three times. You are at home in your body.

Fear

Fear is a natural, powerful, and primitive human emotion. It involves a universal biochemical response as well as a highly individual emotional response. Fear alerts us to the presence of danger or the threat of harm, whether that danger is physical or psychological.

Fear, not hate, is the opposite of love. Hate actually requires an emotional attachment to another person, so it's just a dark version of love, like obsession or infatuation. Fear is its own emotion; it is the sensation of the ego that we have to fight off in order to act or **do** just about anything worthwhile.

Fear is primitive, as is love. Both are innate human emotions. We are born with a love attachment to our mothers, who carried us in the womb for the better part of a year, as well as to others who feed and care for us. We are also born with a fear of death, fear of being dropped or falling. So, as fear alerts us to threats or danger, love lets us know that we are safe and protected. These two emotions form the root of all other emotional branches. For example, fear-based sadness is hopelessness, a fear that the world is unsafe and unloving and we are unloved. Love-based sadness is heartbreak/grief, the overwhelming feeling of not being able to send and share love with another being or never having experienced unconditional love at all. That experience makes the world and even life feel scary.

Our greatest challenge is to be able to identify a real threat when fear arises and then choose love for all other challenges, obstacles, and tasks. This statement is not meant to diminish the feelings of someone suffering from depression, anxiety, or PTSD. As a fellow member of this club, I have struggled with this challenge for years and consider it part of my ongoing journey. On the days that I go deep into the divine light in me and have faith in myself, the earth and the universe to support me and keep me alive. And I choose love. We can practice asking ourselves:

- Is this fear valid?
- Do I have control over the outcome?

- What is the worst possible outcome?
- Is the worst possible outcome that bad?
- What is the best possible outcome?
- How great would that be?
- Can I see myself in the future living that outcome?
- How does that look?
- Do I love myself enough to do this, despite the fear?

Around 99 percent of the time, we fear potential good outcomes as much as the bad, because we doubt ourselves or our worth. We are worthy of many things. And when we achieve something, we help others directly or indirectly. We can find our way back from many detours if we adhere to the cycle of Grace, Gratitude, and Generosity. Some days it's all about being generous with ourselves, having gratitude for our opportunities, and living a life in grace. Sometimes it's about being graceful and allowing someone else to be generous with us, to help us, to support us, to love us, and to have gratitude for their effort and compassion.

When we let go of self-judgment, we naturally let go of the impulse to judge others. When we release fear, anger, and resentment, and instead, love ourselves unconditionally, we can go with the flow and live in a balanced state of abundance and worthiness more easily. We as spiritual beings have the power to create heaven on earth and live compassionate and peaceful lives. It doesn't have to be just a fantasy in a movie or a song; it is possible. We can do many amazing things when we put love into them.

Releasing Fear

I do not allow anger or anxiety to take over.
Instead, I sink into the feelings
and uncover why I'm anxious, afraid, or angry.
I am in a safe space.
This space is being held for me to be vulnerable and
honest, and to heal.
I surround myself with love, compassion, and forgiveness.
I carry love with me everywhere.
I allow love to be the companion to every other emotion
And I love myself through it.
All of these feelings are temporary.
I am not defined by my "broken" parts.
I am whole and beautiful.
I am strong, safe, and grounded.
I am brave in the face of fear.
I am healing.
I am letting go.
I release all fear.
I am not my emotions.
I am perfectly me.
I embrace all that I am, light and dark.
I embrace strength;
I own it.
I embrace peace;
I resonate with it.
I embrace love; I am love.
I am everything that is.
I am all that I am.
I got this!

Chapter 5

Sacral Chakra & Creative Energy

"Creativity has got to start with humanity
and when you're a human being,
you feel, you suffer."
– Marilyn Monroe

The Sacral Chakra

The second chakra is orange, Svadhisthana in Sanskrit. This is the physical space of our reproductive system as well as the energetic source of fertility and of creative and sexual energy. When aligned, we are fertile with feminine, creative energy, even men. We are passionate and comfortable with our sexuality.

The fifth dimensional aspect of the sacral chakra not only concerns our sexuality but also how we relate to others. All of our ancestral trauma, ancestral DNA, and family relationships, such as resentment or our role as the breaker of traumatic patterns and chains, tend to be formed and perhaps even stored in this chakra.

At the area just below our navel is our energetic source creation point. In Reiki, we call it the Seat of Reiki. In yoga and Chinese medicine, they call it the conception vessel. It is, energetically, where all life force begins. It is the base point of our connection to source. All of our creative energy is birthed there. Our imagination, or third eye, is definitely part of our creative process. Many know that our throat chakra is part of our creative expression, but the start of our feminine creative life force begins right below the spot where your umbilical cord once fed you all that you needed to be born.

Creativity

I release the karmic chains of fear and self-doubt.
I let go with love and forgive all in my past
that planted seeds of doubt, guilt, or shame.
I am brave and strong.
I am centered and balanced on my journey
through this life!
I am free!
I gracefully and graciously accept, embrace,
and celebrate all of my blessings and talents.
I bravely share my talents and gifts with others
So that we may all rise up to be our greatest selves!
I trust in myself.
I am grounded.
I am safe.
I am ready to shine once again and light my own stage.
I AM!

Manifestation

Manifestation is not: "An unexpected $10,000 will arrive in your bank account in the next 24 hours."

Manifestation is:

- Recognizing our self-worth.
- Embracing our light and dark.
- Knowing what our burning desire is.
- Confidently believing our worth for this outcome and knowing 100 percent that it already exists at some time in the future.
- Using creative source as a womb for birthing positive energy, nourished by our wishes, desires, or ideas.
- Setting the goal and then taking steps every day.
- Recognizing that the inner critic is not our truth but the embodiment of all the negative programming we have received from parents, teachers, and elders. It's time to let the lies go.
- Acknowledging the cheerleaders in our head, heart, and gut; they know what's going on and that we are worthy!
- AND taking action to achieve it, trusting that it (or something even better) has already actualized in the future!
- Living that self-actualization in the present tense, because we **know** it is already so!
- That is how the Law of Attraction really works and what this book, essentially, is about. Set the world on fire with our potential and all we are! The world is waiting for us to be and live our truth!

Manifest the F*ck Out of Your Life!

I release all energy of doubt and unworthiness.
I release all limiting beliefs and programming from all
sources of fear or negativity.
Fuck the haters and the critics!
I forgive the judgment; it is not mine to pick up.
I reclaim my power over my creativity
and free myself from any creative blocks.
I embrace all the creative energy
and feminine passion within me.
I embrace my quirks and my weird as well as my strengths;
I am exactly who I need to be.
I am worthy of my dreams!
The world needs me and the creations I share.
I look forward with hope, confidence, and purpose.
I am safe and steady.
I am here for a reason.
I am inspired!
I visualize what I want and place it safely,
surrounded by love, in the future.
I know it is so then and take steps every day
to bring myself closer to that truth.
I am confident that talent, faith, and work
will bring my desired outcome or better,
as the universe sees fit.
I am ready to share all of my gifts and my true self
with the world,
so that we may all rise up to be our greatest selves
and fill the world with love and light!

Our Soul Family

Believe it or not, we choose our parents. I'm sorry to be the truth teller, but yes, it's true. We tend to pick a similar group of souls to incarnate with to overcome past karma or help each other grow. The same is true of our potential children. Whether we choose to have children or not, the souls of our potential children in this lifetime are around us.

Our ancestral line is linked for at least three generations from the get-go. The egg that created each of us was formed in our mothers' ovaries in our grandmothers' wombs. Fact. All of our souls spend time together in the collective of heaven. We make an agreement or soul contract with each other before we're born, choosing who will be mother, father, sister, brother, etc., and wait until it's our turn to arrive.

Each of us knows going in that there is the potential for miscarriage, termination, fertility issues, or free will that leads our parents to choose not to have children. In any of these cases, those spirit children are still soul contracted to be in our lives. They serve as our guardian angels, teachers, and guides in body or spirit. Each child is not only someone we raise, teach, and guide, but they also teach us a lot about ourselves and help us realize our higher purpose. They are little mirrors and reflections of the things we say, how we treat others, and what we are truly like. They love us unconditionally and give us the perfect opportunity to see ourselves with that same unconditional love and acceptance.

Whether they make it to human form or not, our spirit children are always with us. Women know this better than anyone, because we feel the presence of our children before we even try to conceive. They are attached to the eggs that were formed in our mothers' wombs, waiting patiently for the perfect time. They know better than any of us about when they will come, their sex, and even what they will look like; and sometimes they even choose their own name and telepathically whisper it to us before we're even old enough to procreate. Ladies, did you write a list of baby names in your teens? Mm-hmm, me too. Our biological clock starts ticking really loud when one of them is getting ready to come. It's not just biological; this is our karmic soul blueprint overlapping theirs. It's time.

The following is helpful to create and hold the energetic space for children to go from a concept and an egg to a potential baby. Each soul has free will. As much as I can see of a person's past or future, I cannot predict if a baby will be born, born unhealthy, or miscarried. There are so many factors involved. That said, clearing karmic and unworthiness baggage and replacing it with positivity and fertile energy has helped many people I've worked with. This affirmation can also be used for creative professionals and anyone working on connecting with their feminine energy.

Creativity & Fertility

I release all doubt.
I release all vibration of fear.
I release all feelings of less-than and unworthy.
I release all energy of anger and jealousy.
I have all that I need.
I am safe.
I am whole.

I embrace my feminine energy.
I am a creator!
I am bountiful with creative energy.
I love the sensation of creation.
I am pregnant with potential new beginnings.
I embrace my curves and edges.
I am sexy and oozing with femininity.
I am desired.
I am a beautiful expression and manifester of humanity!
I am a nurturer.
I am fertile.
I am worthy of creative inspiration
and the gift of creation.

I am free from all the baggage
of other people's judgments.
I am free of the chains that hold me back.
I am worthy.
I am enough.
I am loved.

(continued…)

I am love.
I love.
I love life.
I create life.
I am the co-creator of my own life!
I am a goddess.
I am perfect as I am.

Perfection

Every baby born seems to be perfect. We even say it about them as we marvel over their small, helpless bodies. We are born exactly as we are meant to be in order to "become" the person we intend to be, once we overcome our karma and any tasks or lessons we intend to learn. We choose our parents out of all the potential souls in the world so that they can help us be who and what we need to be in this or that lifetime. We even select both the egg and the sperm that we want to merge to create the physical form that we are meant to be to help us become an even better, more elevated version of ourselves.

Our unique being is perfectly imperfect. The ideal we hold about perfection is an illusion, because each of us is exactly as we are supposed to be when we arrive and to become the adult we're supposed to be. Birds don't sit in judgment of their different colors. Trees care for sick trees so that all of them can thrive. There is beauty in the broken, imperfect, and wild. Height, eye color, learning disability, or chronic illness are not flaws. All of these aspects of ourselves are delicately considered as tools for us to reach our highest vibration possible each lifetime. Why is it so challenging for us to see the beauty in our own battle scars? If our souls wanted an easy life, we would have stayed in heaven. Life on earth is challenging and exciting! We get to feel the broad range of emotions and physical experiences. Look life in the eye and say, "Yes!"

I am perfectly imperfect.
I am all that I am,
light and dark.
I am perfectly me.

Chapter 6

Solar Plexus Chakra: Confidence & Willpower

"Success is liking yourself, liking what you do, and liking how you do it."
– Maya Angelou

Solar Plexus & Self-Confidence

The solar plexus chakra, or Manipura, vibrates at a yellow frequency and represents our ego, self-esteem, willpower, personal power, free will, and autonomy/independence. Often, when things seem completely out of control, this is the chakra we need to look at.

When this chakra is out of balance, we have low self-confidence, and addiction issues. We may also have a complete lack of ambition. On the flipside, our imbalance may cause us to act out rather than inward and abuse power or try to control or overpower others. This is a chakra, as well as the crown and heart chakra, where depression or anxiety can manifest. When in balance, we are confident and considerate; we feel that we are worthy and enough.

At the fifth dimensional level of this chakra, all of our wisdom is held and will transfer from subconscious/spiritual to conscious/physical as we are ready to receive it. It's like an energetic receptor or feeler of vibrations in the universe. This chakra can be a beacon of light to others on a subconscious level, and we empaths may feel things in this upper-abdominal "gut" when things are amiss or out of balance in ourselves, in others, in the world, or in the universe.

Just for Today

Just for today, I believe in myself.
Just for today, I love with all my heart.
Just for today, I love myself.
Just for today, I release all fear and shame.

Just for today, I release all the hurt and hate.
Just for today, I am forgiving.
Just for today, I release all that doesn't serve
my healing and wellness.
My well-being is my highest purpose…
Just for today.

It's All Good

Sometimes we ignore the reality of who we truly are. We may discover a skill that feels so natural, we wonder how we know it. We have access to so much more wisdom than our conscious mind knows. The wisdom of our souls, the cellular DNA of our ancestors, lives in our bodies, and the wisdom of our past lives resides in our souls. We each hold a set of keys to the universe and they unlock doors that help each of us live the best possible life. It's easy to get frustrated and impatient, but 99.99 percent of the time, everything is in Divine Time and we just can't see or understand that in the present moment. Stay true to yourself, be brave, and try things that scare you, especially if you think you might enjoy them or be good at them! Life is joy! We choose to come back again and again to enjoy the journey back home to the truest and purest version of ourselves. We are meant to confidently enjoy the adventure. Get out there and live your best life!

All of Me

I release all self-doubt.
I release all limiting beliefs.
I release all guilt and shame.
I release all energy of blame.
I lovingly let go of all emotional, mental,
and karmic baggage
that no longer serves me or my growth.

I am not broken; I am whole!
I am perfectly imperfect.
I am special in my sensitivity.
I am powerful beyond my own belief!

I trust myself.
I trust in the universe that I am safe.
I AM safe.

I am lovable.
I am unconditionally loved.
I love myself at all ages of my life.
I support my growth through self-love and self-confidence.
I believe in ME!
I am healing.
I AM!

Acceptance in the Present Moment

Today, I am strong.
I embrace my inner strength.
Today, I am also vulnerable and sensitive.
I surrender to all of it and hold a space for me to feel.
I am safe in my vulnerability.
I am enough just as I am.
The purest essence of me will always be.
All other changes are expansions, improvements,
and upgrades.
I speak my truth with purpose, confidence, bravery,
and compassion.
I recognize that every ending is a new beginning.
Energy never dies;
it only transforms.
All will be revealed in Divine Time, with faith.
I trust and have faith in myself.
I am that I AM.

Worthiness

Every human being, every soul is worthy of compliments and praise when we have done well and are worthy of compassion when we have not. I will not get into a deep discussion of abusers or murderers, but I will say this: Someone loves or loved them too. No one is born a murderer or abuser; something happened to them in order to point them in such a dark, fearful, and angry direction. When it comes to this depth of darkness, we can strive to hold a space for compassion for the child or the soul that has been pushed or led down a dark path of lies and abuse to believe that is okay. When we hold a space in this way, we don't burden ourselves with hate and then that negativity cannot harm us.

This book (and life) is all about choosing love, kindness, and compassion, as well as ending the cycles of self-sabotage, criticism, and neglect! Being able to give and receive is linked to many other aspects of our healing and both seeing and speaking our truth. Being grounded and balanced helps us give and receive with balance. One good deed deserves praise or reward. When we are able to stand in grace, we can be generous and grateful. This level of balance, perfect balance, is the harmony that the world is heading toward and will thrive in. If we can each manifest perfect harmony with ourselves, we can do the same with one another as well. Manifest balance! You're so worth it!

I Am Worthy

I am here in this world right now.
I am steady and grounded,
supported by the earth,
in perfect physical balance with the force of gravity
and my soul's will.
I am in harmony in body, mind, and soul,
connected to both heaven and earth.
I feel my worthiness.
I am worthy of having my place on this planet.
I am worthy of the air I breathe and the food I eat.
I am worthy of life.
I am valued by all my guides, guardians,
and loved ones in heaven
and all those who love me and know me on earth.
I am worthy of compliments.
I am worthy of generosity.
I am worthy of whatever form
of recognition and reciprocation
is fit from another person.
When I accept their compliments or gifts,
I honor their worth.
I graciously accept all of it.
Thank you for seeing me.
I welcome validation, but I do not live to seek it.
I am thankful and fulfilled.
I am living an abundant life,
filled with unconditional love, friendship,
and work I enjoy.
I am living my best life!
I generously share compliments and smiles

(continued…)

without fear or hesitation.
I offer assistance when I am able,
without expectation of reward or validation.
I am generous, because I am human.
Kindness and compassion are my religion.
I drop any judgment of myself or others
and pay the energy of abundance forward.
I live my life in the vibration of unconditional love.
I am steady, grounded, and supported.
I am perfectly me.
I AM.

Gratitude, Grace, & Generosity

I once channeled a message from the angels that said there are three vibrations of energy that are vital to a happy and well-lived life: grace, gratitude, and generosity. Each of these has a very similar frequency and a thread that connects them. They can be practiced and experienced simultaneously or separately, but they each hold a value of connection to others. This belief that we are all spiritually linked in a collective human vibration, a spiritual energy that links us to every living thing on this earth, helps us to realize gratitude, grace, and generosity.

Once we find our balance and start loving and liking ourselves, we can find balance in giving and receiving. When we believe we are unworthy of unconditional love, we believe we are unworthy of so many things. We believe we are unworthy of praise, compliments, gifts, or any form of generosity.

Gratitude: Appreciation and thankfulness.

When we are grateful for what we have, we have fewer feelings of wanting, longing, or "less-than" mindset. With gratitude comes a feeling of "I am enough" and "I have enough." It is a place of peace, balance, and contentment. I have everything I need.

Gratitude is essential in attitude alignment and healing. If we don't appreciate the things, beings, and experiences around us or ourselves, we cannot truly heal or live a good life without gratitude.

Gratitude

I am grateful for the sun.
I am grateful for the bees.
I am grateful for the moon.
I am grateful for the trees.
I am grateful for the mountains.
I am grateful for the sea.
I am grateful for you.
I am grateful for me.

Generosity: Giving to ourselves, as well as others, with love and without expectation of something in return.

When we have gratitude and feel we have everything we need, we experience a state of contented serenity. We often feel moved to share and give back or pay it forward to those that have less. The true human condition is wanting everyone to be okay and have enough. Humane means having or showing compassion or benevolence. We are born wanting to share. Babies and children naturally share. Yes, toddlers go through a "mine" phase, but that is natural and normal in human development as they must learn to gain a sense of autonomy. What is abnormal is the continued behavior of greed or jealousy into adulthood. The more thankful we are, the more generous we feel and have the capacity to be.

Generosity

I live an abundant life.
I have enough.
I am enough.
I am whole.
When I can share a smile, love, food, clothing, or shelter
without expectation of reciprocity,
I am fulfilled in my soul.
There is a constant flow of energy.
I share out of love.
I live my life in love.
I am fulfilled and abundant with love.
I am generous with love and grace.
I am generous with myself and to others.

Which leads us to grace...

Grace: the state of being thoughtful or considerate; in good favor; the absolute balance, the quiet, calm contentment in perfect balance between generosity and gratitude.

This is the balance we seek. This is true inner peace that we can find in life. It is a state of fulfilment. There are so many definitions of the word grace that no matter how you interpret the word, it is positive and beautiful! This is something that we can each work toward; the path to that grace is gratitude and generosity.

Grace

I am grateful for all of my blessings and gifts.
I am grateful for all of my perceived flaws and have faith
that their value
will be revealed in Divine Time.
I am grateful for all the people in my life
who love and accept me unconditionally.
I am grateful for all that I am.

I express gratitude, with generosity of my heart.
I compliment my friends and family.
I acknowledge strangers when I observe their generosity
and when they look like they need words of
encouragement.
I share my gifts with others, generously.
I recognize that my gifts were meant to be shared.
I encourage others to share their gifts.
I generously pay positive energy forward,
in smiles, in money, in hugs, in time…

I walk my life's path with grace and balance.
I gracefully accept my karma and all the contracts
that I have chosen to fulfill.
I am gracious in receiving guidance, advice, and
support from my guardian angels and earth angels.
I graciously accept compliments and offerings as the
blessings they are.
I choose to live my life
with grace, gratitude, and generosity.

Trigger Warning: This chapter contains affirmations and exercises to help face our shadows. The notion of "shadows" can refer to trauma, dysfunctional family issues, and anything else in our past that may be stored as negative energy, self-sabotage, pain, or illness in the body, mind, or soul.

Chapter 7

Embracing Our Light, Dark, & Shades of Gray

"Everyone carries a shadow, and the less it is embodied in the individual's conscious life, the blacker and denser it is. If an inferiority is conscious, one always has a chance to correct it. Furthermore, it is constantly in contact with other interests, so that it is continually subjected to modifications. But if it is repressed and isolated from consciousness, it never gets corrected."
– Carl Jung, *Psychology and Religion*

The Shadow

The famous Swiss psychoanalyst Carl Jung emphasized in his work that part of understanding all aspects of ourselves means facing our light and dark, or "shadow" aspects. This does not mean that our aspects are black and white or right and wrong. Most of us have thought, at times, that certain aspects of ourselves are ugly or unacceptable. We bag or box those parts up and carry them around obliviously or in shame while they negatively affect or sabotage all of our relationships from then on. But we can do what is called "shadow work." Shadow work has two categories:

- Being honest with ourselves about our shadow
- Embracing the shadow events in our lives.

Most of us go through life with our shadow living in our subconscious mind. We don't acknowledge or address it and sometimes we are so blind to it that we cannot even recognize our own truth. Many of us have qualities that are less than flattering or that we see in others but not ourselves. That truth always includes our shadow.

For example, you might know someone who constantly complains about a parent, friend, or sister acting in particular way and you quietly think, "You do that all the time, bro!" They don't recognize their own shadow! They cannot see, recognize, or accept this aspect of themselves, so the universe sends them a mirror to help them see it and work with it. Every time one of our relatives or friends does something that annoys us, that we actually do too, we're being given an opportunity to face and embrace our shadow. This is a big aspect of the work we must do to find inner peace and contentment. Without embracing the shadow, we're living a lie. When we finally say, "Oh wow! I do that!" we can forgive when someone else does it to us, because we suddenly have compassion for them and ourselves. We can apologize, ask for forgiveness, and give it as well.

The shame aspect of shadow also consists of the limiting beliefs we were told when we were little from our parents and other authority figures. Behaviors and actions our parents modeled for us become normalized, whether they are appropriate or not. Their actions become part of our conscious and unconscious truth, which are actually lies we believe about ourselves as a result of trauma or dysfunction that we suffered. Some of us take in and repress unacceptable behavior and messages. As children, we don't have the maturity to recognize the reality, so we rationalize or integrate abuse. Later, it evolves into abandonment anxiety or we carry shame about things that happened to us, including abuse, trauma, or illness that we have no control over. It is buried in our subconscious, but until we face and embrace it, as adults, it trickles into everything we do and, especially, how we feel about ourselves.

Every single one of us must go through this shadow work if we want to live a balanced life and attract the best possible partner to love, grow, and evolve with. We can fall in love with someone without doing shadow work, but we generally attract the mirror we need to see our true selves and then move on if that person no longer fits. If we believe these lies of shame, we will only attract people that reinforce and validate that shame and stay there, because that's what we think we deserve.

A discussion of shadow work could be an entire book, so this chapter just scratches the surface. The purpose here is to begin to look at all of you, light and dark. Whatever we perceive about ourselves that we think is ugly or unbecoming is still part of the self. Each of us must look at the big picture and love ourselves without judgment in order to live with a light heart.

Shadow Work Exercise

Take a little time to write down the things you love about yourself and then the things you don't like.

Like/Light	Don't Like/Shadow
_____	_____
_____	_____
_____	_____
_____	_____
_____	_____
_____	_____
_____	_____
_____	_____
_____	_____

Which list is longer? Take a look at that shadow list. Cross off all the things on that list that are out of your control, for example, your eye color, your height, the color of your skin, and anything else that is physical. Those are merely your skin suit, the avatar you chose in this lifetime. They is not who you are. You are your soul. The body is just the costume you chose.

Next, look at the soul and personality traits you listed under shadow. Can you put a positive spin on any of them? For example, if you're controlling, can you embrace the fact that you are a great planner or have great leadership skills? If this is something people complain about, then it's something to look at. Anything that people judge about you is a good place to start. Sometimes they are dealing with their shadow and seeing or misconstruing your truth, but often, it's a great place to start.

Let's stick with controlling as an example. What led to that? No baby is born controlling. What happened that made you feel out of control? Sit with the feelings that pop up with that memory for a bit. You are safe in your body. You are safe in your mind. You are safe right now. It is safe to feel. Allow the light to shine on your shadows right now. Breathe. Cry if you need to. Hug yourself. Love yourself.

As a result of your history, you are controlling. Surrender to that. Embrace that about yourself. Give up trying to "fix" it. You are how you are. For this moment, right now, love yourself exactly as you are.

Once we embrace the things in ourselves that irritate us about others, they have less power. The reason we were bothered by that other person's behavior is because we secretly hated that aspect of ourselves. Other times, things bother us because of trauma or shame. We don't want to look at these things, so we judge them in others. Instead of realizing that we are regimented and like things a certain way as a coping mechanism for a chaotic childhood, we often see that aspect in someone else and judge or shame them for being the exact same way. Many of us go through our entire lives never dealing with our shadow at all. We carry the guilt, shame or ignorance that we have anything negative or unkind to "fix" at all. To clarify, the trait is not negative and not necessarily something to fix, but instead, it is the "closet door" to be opened to deal with the past event, behavior, memory or experience that caused it. Once the light shines on our shadow and we see the whole self, soulfully naked and true, that aspect of shadow or that trauma we experienced no longer has power over us. For most of us, this little bit of shadow work can be life altering.

Just for Today

Just for today…
I release all self-doubt.
I release all feelings of less-than.
I release all limiting beliefs.
I release all energy of unlovable.
I am worthy.
I am lovable.
I am loved.
I am whole.
I am complete.
I am enough.
I embrace all that I am,
light and dark,
with unconditional love.

"The two wolves in me are not at war.
In fact, they are lovers.
The black wolf is powerful and reckless
and howls at the moon.
The white wolf is spiritual and kind
and prefers bathing under the sun.
They are polar opposites; therefore,
they are the perfect pair.
I feed them both. I control them both."
 – a. r. lucas

Embrace Your Light and Dark

We each have a potential for light and dark within us. Like a yin-yang symbol, nothing is completely or inherently good or bad, black or white; everything just is and the contrast is needed for us to "see" clearly. We all have talents and flaws. We have a variety of colors or shades of emotions and feelings! This is what makes life interesting! Everything is shades of gray or potential possible outcomes; nothing is so concrete. However, energetically, we refer to light and dark when referring to energy or traits that we assign as positive or negative. When we attach shame to our emotions or abuse, it becomes dark or shadowy. In truth, shame is fear of judgment or our response to judgment. That "creates" the darkness that's wrapped around our energy field. Our so-called negative or dark parts are just as beautiful and necessary for us to become the best possible version of ourselves. Judgment is the dirty word here. When we judge others or ourselves, that is the shadow.

We have to find the balance, the harmony, and make peace between our light and dark. Once we do, we will live a happier life. The lows will feel like a bump in the road, filled with lessons. The highs will help us embrace others in joy and feel our oneness! Each of us can say, "I am perfectly me," and mean it. Even if there are things we want to improve, fix, or tweak, right now, you are perfectly you as you are meant to be at this moment, on this planet, in this universe.

Experiences—great, awful, and in-between—change us. They carve out pathways in our brains, in our bodies, in our souls. Who I am now can look back at what seemed like an insignificant experience and say, "That is totally fucking relevant to what is going on in my life right now!" When we live our lives without regret, a traumatic or challenging experience can remind us how strong we are and help us realize our potential. Past events I've had often help me guide Reiki healing energy to exactly where it is needed for a person suffering from a similar vibration, and that wisdom and energy of collective understanding and care helps them release the stored negative energy to start healing. Instead of living in regret, we can transmute that negative into positive of "How can I do better in my present life?"

Trauma, like grief, may stay with us for our entire existence. But love does too! The less we try to hide our trauma or our pain, the less power it has over us. When I was 19, I was raped. This book is not about my journey through that, but a lot of what is in this book are ways I worked through all of my obstacles and trauma. I regret nothing. If that terrifying event didn't happen, I would not have gone to therapy so young, worked through that along with family dysfunction. I am who I am today, because of all I have experienced and overcome. I'm not ready to go thank the person who raped me, but I'm also far beyond carrying guilt or shame when I had every right to feel safe in my body. I am surely not a blip on his conscience. Therefore, there is no reason for me or any of us to carry the baggage of abuse, trauma, neglect, narcissism, or shame. We do not deserve that and we aren't here for that.

We are here to realize our greatest potential, to manifest happiness. When we focus on loving ourselves, we feed the energy of compassion and kindness. We bring that to the surface and we're able to free ourselves from the pain and fear. We never stop loving someone we care about, even with their flaws, so why is it so hard to embrace our own light and dark?

There may come a time when we wake up and realize that the things we feared or were ashamed of about ourselves are actually gifts. Our perceived flaws were actually a superpower all along! Without fear, we might never move out of a bad situation. Without anger, we might not change. We are the sum of all our parts, and that is the beauty of humanity.

Affirm out loud:

I embrace all that I am!

We must say it every day until we mean it and then say it until we are living it so much that other people notice. Allow everything within to balance out. Namaste (the light and dark in me recognizes the light and dark in you!).

I Embrace All That I Am

I breathe in and embrace
all that is light and dark
within me.
I embrace all the shades of my personality and my soul.
I breathe out and release
all self-judgment...fear...shame.
I am filled with and surrounded by infinite,
unconditional love.
I forgive and let go of all that keeps me
from fully loving myself.
I am thankful for the lessons.
I appreciate and embrace all the quirks and qualities that I
viewed as flaws.
Without them, I would not be me.
I accept and love all that I am, inside and out,
light and dark.
I am perfectly imperfect.
I am perfectly me!

Trauma & Post-Traumatic Stress Disorder (PTSD)

If we're talking about shadow and battle scars, then we have to address trauma. There is no benefit or glory to suffering. Hiding trauma in our energetic closet does not make us stronger. Shame attacks us to our physical, mental, emotional, and spiritual core. Sometimes the wounds are so deep that we live in the vibration of trauma for years or even decades. Trauma makes us anxious, fearful, and sometimes angry. Healing makes us stronger. We may be left with scars, but over time, we can recognize the value of the scars rather than the trauma of the awful experience.

In the energy healing work that I do, I work with a great deal of individuals who have had trauma. The statistics vary, but it is thought that between one in four or one in three women have been sexually assaulted. Many men have also been abused and assaulted. Unfortunately, I have known many trauma survivors of both genders. Overcoming the fear, anger, depression, or anxiety of trauma is truly beautiful to witness and makes us incredibly strong.

It's not an easy process and we have to pull out all of our emotional baggage, like Marie Kondo, and sift through each piece. Like Kondo asks, "What sparks joy?" What are you proud of? What do you not like about yourself in this present moment? Is it something you can work on? Great! You have some work to do. If it's not, shine a light on it and decide if it's really as ugly as you think. Is this something that makes you who you are? If you got rid of it, would you no longer be you?

Perhaps it's time to take a deep breath and embrace the things we don't like as much as the things we love about ourselves. Together, all the pieces make who we are today.

The scars of trauma, like grief, might stay with us for a while. But love does too! We never stop loving someone we care about, even with their flaws. Our trauma scars are often only detected by others with similar scars and we see each other like no one else can. We help each other grow by holding a mirror up to each other to see our own inner beauty through each other's eyes. We can say:

I see you.
I believe you.
You are so much more than that thing
that happened to you.
Embrace your own light and dark!
Wear your battle scars with pride!
This is what you have overcome.

Clear & Protect Your Energy Field

I release all that does not serve me.
I release all pain, hurt, and trauma.
I cast out all the shadows that keep me
from moving forward.
I liberate all darkness that has kept me in fear.
I shine light on all the contrast
of my shame, guilt, and pain.
None of it is for my greatest good;
It is not mine to carry
and no one can hurt me again.
That was then.
I am safe now.
I am stronger. I am strong!
I am protected.
I am not my past.
I am who and what I choose to be.
I am not broken.
I am healing.
My scars make me stronger.
Wiser.
I am safe in my boundaries.
I am surrounded by light and love.
I love myself unconditionally.
I am all that I am.
I AM!

Finding Beauty in the Broken

The indelible print that trauma leaves on our souls, in our memory, and even in our bodies is something we can't erase, but we can heal with help and support. When we are traumatized, we often feel completely alone. We are never alone! Even if we are distant from people physically, there is a tribe of people who care about us and spirit guides and guardian angels are with us at every moment. There is always an angel just a prayer or thought away. Though they cannot intervene, they can support and protect our souls. At the core of our soul, we are always safe and we are connected to all the energy in the universe. Each of us has a divine glowing light inside that no one can ever harm. Can you imagine the visual of that? All the souls in the universe lit up like candles or a blanket of stars across the galaxies. Beautiful, right? Our souls are beautiful and there is beauty in our scars.

The Japanese believe that our scars are beautiful and should not be hidden. Kintsugi is the art of enhancing and preserving the breaks in pottery, just as our own "cracks" and scars in life make us more interesting, beautiful, and stronger once we heal. We are beautiful.

All the healing in the world begins with love. All of our learning experiences must pass through the heart. Life is filled with all the emotions. In order to learn and grow, we must feel. Though the process is painful, the outcome is beautiful. Love is the key. When we are suffering, broken, or out of balance, it's hard to see the best in ourselves; love can break through that. A snuggle from a cat. A hug from Mom. These are healing to our souls. The people closest to us get to see all sides: happy, sad, angry, scared. They love us unconditionally. When we are in a healthy, balanced state, we can also love ourselves unconditionally. We can see that all aspects of ourselves are beautiful; even the cracked or broken pieces can become beautiful.

The Universal Life Force that is Reiki is like unconditional love, and that level of energy heals! Reiki and talk therapy complement each other very well in relation to depression, anxiety, and PTSD. I've had therapists recommend their clients with PTSD to me and I've recommended my clients to therapists. Trauma is multidimensional in the body-mind-soul, the same way our memories are stored in the brain and in the cells within our body. A smell, a sound, a touch can trigger a traumatic memory and the body-mind-soul responds. The energy of the traumatic event can lie dormant in our hips, our heart, our bellies, or wherever the trauma affected us. Together, Reiki and talk therapy have a way of releasing and clearing the heightened reaction and pain involved in the stress and anxiety of chronic post-traumatic stress disorder. Some clients say that Reiki saved their lives.

I believe that we can only heal from trauma with help. We need the support of at least one impartial and available person to be part of a collective to hear us, nurture us, and direct us toward empowerment. When we are stuck in the fog of shame or self-doubt caused by trauma, it's challenging to see the truth—that we are loved, lovable, and worthy of love. We must find effective professionals/therapists/healers in order to move beyond the trauma. At the early part of my healing journey, after my own sexual trauma, I was in group therapy. It was the most supportive environment because I knew I wasn't alone. Years later, yoga and Reiki helped me work through the darkest, deepest buried aspects of it. We are always whole, but we need to hold a space for ourselves even if we are not ready to look at all of our trauma, karma, or drama. A professional can help us do this in our own time.

When looking for a therapist or energy healer, I encourage you to do your research about him or her. Find a therapist who specializes[1] or has special training with PTSD (post-traumatic stress disorder), sexual trauma, depression, addiction, or ADHD. Often trauma-specialized professionals have EMDR (Eye Movement Desensitization and Reprocessing)[2] or TMS (Transcranial Magnetic Stimulation) training, which can be effective for many. EMDR is a very specific technique for helping people with trauma to reconnect to the images, emotions and physical sensations associated with the

---

[1] https://www.childtrauma.com/blog/find-good-therapist

[2] https://www.emdria.org/

trauma, while working with the natural self-healing powers of the brain to resolve these triggers. TMS is another non-invasive technique to help people suffering from depression, using magnetic pulses, like those of an MRI. The magnetic energy stimulates the mood receptors in the brain, activates new cell growth as well as neurotransmitters, like serotonin, dopamine and norepinephrine without the side effects of antidepressants. Always ask a potential therapist about their techniques and how they would help someone like you. When researching a Reiki or other energy healers, ask them about their training and philosophy.

- Are they a Reiki Master?
- Do they have experience working with trauma?
- Do they practice self-healing or self-care?
- How do they keep their own energy field clear?

If it doesn't feel right, it's not right. It is so challenging for us to trust our post-traumatic selves, but we must trust if something doesn't feel right. However, if we're denying ourselves out of fear, that's another story. If we have a "funny feeling" about someone that makes us not trust, we must honor that. If we are afraid of remembering or feeling the pain again, that's different. Healing is hard. Living with the pain and stored trauma is harder, uglier, and much more painful and scary than bringing childhood abuse, neglect, and trauma into the light. It feels like the Hallelujah Chorus when there's a breakthrough!

I believe that we can tell if a professional is right for us in the first 30 to 60 seconds of a conversation or phone call. Does that person make us feel safe? Do they have a soothing and authentic vocal tone? Are they talking to me with compassion and asking the questions I need someone to ask? The people who help us the most have compassion, a love and honesty about the work they do. Choose those people and there's a better chance of finding the truth and ending suffering. Suffering silently keeps us from our greatest potential. Seek help. Each of us deserves a good life!

The strongest and most beautiful people I know have been through something difficult, painful, or even horrific. In time, with healing, each of us can learn to embrace the damage of our past and emerge in glorious beauty. Someday, each of us will be faced with a moment when we can share the truth about our past and that sharing will help someone else to also be brave, trust, and heal. Then we heal together as a collective, manifesting unconditional love all over this planet!

IF YOU ARE IN CRISIS, CALL:

The National Sexual Assault Hotline: 1-800-656-4673 or **The Suicide Prevention Hotline:** 1-800-273-TALK (8255). If you can't bear to speak about it, but prefer to chat online, RAINN (**rainn.org**) has that option!

And **The Trevor Project/Trevor Lifeline** has three options: 1-866-7386. There is also a chat option and you can reach out by text by texting "Start" to 678-678.

There is help and understanding out there.

Embrace Your Scars—You Are a Beautiful Survivor!

There is beauty in the broken.
There is depth in the imperfect.
There is sanctuary in the wild.
My battle scars, visible and invisible,
are a sign of strength.
Nothing from my past can hurt me again.
I release all that does not serve
my healing and highest purpose.
I am safe.
I am strong.
I am a survivor!
I pick myself up and I fight
for my right to not only exist, but also to live and thrive.
I am important!
My existence is valued.
I am wanted and needed.
I embrace my scars.
I am proud of what I have overcome.
I am not my past.
I am not what has happened to me without my consent.
Starting now, I am who and what I choose to be.
I am strong.
I am healing.
I am whole.
I regret nothing!
I survived!
I am alive!

Coping with a Trigger

Trauma triggers are like allergy attacks. We can't always control them, no matter how prepared we are. How do we manage our allergies? We may have a rescue inhaler, an EpiPen, and/or take medication to prevent or help us manage an allergic reaction. Sometimes there might be an allergy trigger that we can't avoid, particularly if other people aren't aware or did an "oopsie" and used peanut oil to fry the food. The way we crisis-manage that allergy attack is how we have to look at our PTSD/trauma trigger. Our fight, flight, or freeze response has been activated. What do we do? Where's **that** rescue inhaler?

If you've ever watched *Jessica Jones*, you know that the main character repeats words over and over and the viewer doesn't understand them, but it seems to calm her down. This is her coping mechanism, a mindful mantra to manage her panic attacks as a result of her PTSD. She repeats the name of the street and cross streets where she grew up on, perhaps from a time when she felt safe.

This technique is very well known in cognitive behavioral therapy (CBT). Many therapists, even ones who are not extensively trained or certified in PTSD/trauma, are aware of such sensory techniques to help a person ground themselves and find a safe place within.

The problem with trauma is that when we are triggered by something in the present, we are pulled right back into that emotional place and time of fear and helplessness, and the fight, flight, or freeze mechanism is triggered in our brain. In order to gain control back over the body, mind, and emotions, we have to first remember that this is temporary, then come back to the present, ground, and breathe in the now. It can be done with the above technique of repeating words that remind us of positive things, or we can use our senses.

Coping Practice Exercise

Breathe deeply into the bottom of your lungs. **What do you smell?** Nothing? Move on, but keep breathing. Something? Identify the smell and take note of it. Can you bring up a person, place, or thing that has that or a similar smell that helps you feel positive or safe? Continue to breathe.

What do you see? What color is it? Can you find something else of that color? How does that color make you feel? Check in with your body. Is your breath and heart rate slowing down? Keep breathing. Nice and easy.

What do you hear? What is something far away that you can hear? It can be a car engine, a bird singing, children laughing, or rain. It doesn't matter what it is; focus on that sound. Close your eyes if it feels safe and comfortable to do so. If not, drop your eyelids to help you focus on the sound.

Now check in with yourself. **How do you feel?** Can you name the sensations in your body? Can you identify the emotion you're feeling? What color does that feel like? Focus on that color. Breathe in that color in a warm, flowing mist, or a ray of light. Fill the light into your lungs as you breathe in and allow the light to spread around your body as you breathe out. See and feel the warm light traveling down to your feet and glowing past your feet into the earth, like glowing roots of a tree. Feel yourself steady. You are grounded.

Imagine the light glowing brighter and expanding wider around you, like a protective force field or a pillar of light from beneath the ground to the sky. You are safe.

- You are in the present moment.
- Nothing from the past can hurt you now.
- You are not your trauma.
- You are a powerful human being.
- You are sensitive and special.
- You are safe and grounded.
- You are here. Now...

The technique above may be too complicated for some

people. So, there are simplified versions. Another version is to have "favorite" statements ready to go:

Favorite color: *I see purple.*
Favorite sound: *I hear kittens mewing.*
Favorite scent: *I smell roses.*
Favorite taste: *I taste peaches.*
Favorite sensation to feel: *I feel hugs.*

After practicing that for a while and knowing our go-to favorite senses, we can simplify the phrases down to just the word and make it a mantra:

Purple, kittens, roses, peaches, hugs

Sometimes, just hugging ourselves and light patting of our arms can be soothing. When the patting is in an alternating pattern, it actually has neurological benefits. This technique is frequently used with children and, let's face it, we are trying to comfort the child within ourselves in most cases, right?

Freedom from Guilt & Shame

Guilt/shame energy comes from a break in our self-worth and value. When we buy in to the limiting beliefs of society, neglectful or abusive parents, or hurtful teachers or partners, we believe we are less-than and carry around guilt and/or shame. Instead, we have to hold a space for ourselves and drop the guilt and shame and reclaim the power we lost.

Each of us is born powerful, strong, and self-confident. We are each worthy of our own power. We are worthy of all the wisdom and knowledge and love that we seek! We have to believe it. Then, and only then, can we absolutely reclaim our power. Once we own our personal power and space, boundaries will be set and it will be a lot harder to give up our power to anyone else. This is something that each of us must do for ourselves. No healer or therapist can do this for us. They can help facilitate it, hold a space for us, and lead us to the place where, when, and how we can heal; it's very much like Yoda leading Luke Skywalker to the cave and telling him he has to go alone. In the cave, he strikes first against who he thinks is Darth Vader and finds himself under the mask.

The things we loathe in people are often reflections of ourselves, sometimes literally and sometimes figuratively. For example, when we judge someone for being judgy. That's a very clear mirror!

Mirror Work Meditation

When you're ready to take a deeper look at the darker shadows, mirror meditations can help heal some of the trauma or challenges you've faced. Take some alone time for reflecting—cleaning out your emotional closet, attic, and basement, and sitting with your shadows of the past...accepting the now.

Sit in a quiet, comfortable place and position.

Start breathing in a nice balanced pattern, inhaling for a count of four, holding breath in for four, exhaling for four, and holding it out for four. In yoga, we call this balanced breathing or 4-4-4 breath, but it's also known as box breath or box breathing. Do four rounds of that breath to bring yourself to a balanced state.

[PAUSE]

As your body relaxes, notice your mind is clearer, and with each exhalation, release any tension in your body, your shoulders, your jaw, your face.

With closed eyes, imagine yourself in a dimly lit room, sitting at a vanity or a desk with a mirror directly in front of you. Look at yourself. Look deeply into your own eyes. It's okay to giggle or cry if you need to, but keep looking at yourself.

This is a magic mirror. It will serve as a portal that, with the power of your imagination and your subconscious memory bank, will take you on a journey through time.

In your mind, ask the mirror to show you a happy time in your childhood. If you cannot find a happy moment in childhood, I'm sorry you went through that. In that case, dig in to your subconscious to what you imagine a happy childhood would have looked like. Wherever your mind or imagination lands first is perfect. Observe yourself in the mirror. Can you see or imagine how happy you are? Does it make you happy or sad to see yourself then? Take some time to watch your younger self and connect with the joy that you felt at that time. Be as present as you possibly can be with that aspect of yourself in the past.

[PAUSE]

Now imagine your younger self finding a magic mirror and looking in it to see you in the present. How do both of you feel? Sit with the feelings and go back to the 4-4-4 breath if you need to. You are safe. You are always safe. Breathe.

Remember that this mirror is magic. You can speak to the you of your past, and the you from childhood can speak to you. What do you want to say to younger you? You can say anything you like. You can apologize. You can say "I love you." You can talk about the future. Take some time and be with you.

[PAUSE]

As your chat with yourself winds down, little you from the past reaches through the magic mirror and hugs you. Hug yourself back and allow all the emotions and feelings to flow through you. You are safe to feel everything. Feelings cannot harm you. Breathe.

Say farewell for now.

Take some time with the balanced breath once again. A few rounds: inhale for four, hold in for four, exhale for four, and hold out for four.

If you are feeling steady in your emotions and grounded in your body, ask the mirror to bring you back to the past once again. If you are not in a place to continue, keep up with your balanced breathing while hugging yourself and patting your arms in an alternating pattern. You are loved!

[PAUSE]

If you feel ready to take another short journey, your next one will bring you back to a difficult, sad time. You have free will to do this at another time. No one else can choose your path. Remember that you, in the present, are safe. Whatever happened in the past cannot happen to you again. You are grown; you survived and lived on after. The moment you arrive at that moment in the past, greet yourself with compassion and care. Let your younger self know that you are okay now. Reach through the magic mirror and put a hand on your shoulder or hug yourself. You are safe. Tell yourself whatever you wish someone would have said to you then. Sit with yourself for as long as you need. Be with your feelings. You are safe in your feelings. You are safe with yourself. The purest part of yourself is always safe. Keep breathing.

Feel the healing energy of you now with yourself then. Feel how comforted younger you is by your presence and your unconditional love. Feel the mutual love for yourself. You are capable of so much love. You are worthy of all that love. You are loved.

[PAUSE]

Take a deep breath. It's almost time to come back to the present. Remind yourself that you are safe and you are a survivor. With this self-love, you are safe and you are healing.

Before you say farewell, allow the mirror to assist you once more. Ask the mirror to take away anything that does not serve your highest good from the past and the present. Any energy that is not of the highest vibration or light is not worthy to dwell in your body, mind, soul, or home. Let it all go. As it passes through the magic mirror into space, it may be instantly transmuted into positive energy, light, or sent into other dimensions where it will alchemize for millions of years. Whatever happens, you no longer have to carry the burdens that do not serve you and your healing journey.

Thank the mirror for its service and envision yourself covering it with a dark velvet cloak, as if closing this time portal until next time. You may visit and ask for its assistance when you want. Thank anyone else you like, the universe, angels, guides, and guardians for facilitating this exercise, but be sure to thank you.

You have the power to heal yourself. You have the ability to connect with your divine self in any moment of your past and do this exercise.

Return to the breath one last time. Breathe in for a count of four. Hold your breath for a count of four. Exhale for four. Hold your breath out for a count of four.

You are safe. You are balanced. You are grounded and steady. Namaste.

It is best to do this exercise only once a day. It has powerful effects, so it's important to give yourself time to sit with your feelings after a mirror-work journey.

Go Forward Bravely

Look deeply and lovingly at all of your traits, gifts, flaws, and talents. Go deep within. Drop any fear or go forward anyway! Take a leap; walk gingerly; march bravely, but keep moving forward and evolving. Have an open heart and clear mind. Observe. At every present moment, you are at your best and wisest self. No regrets necessary, because you get more and more integrated with your higher self, your divine self, with every decision and step forward, especially the ones that are scary.

This is a journey of reclaiming the power of the self. You have nothing to be ashamed or embarrassed about. Everything just is. Are you ready? Do you believe you are worthy? Okay! Take a deep breath in and repeat the affirmation below with a hand on your heart and seat or feet planted down on a solid surface. You may say this in your mind, but saying it aloud, as any affirmation, amplifies the power of the energy within the words.

I am no longer a survivor or an extra
in my own life story.
I am the protagonist; the hero and I am meant to overcome
all of this bullshit and live my best life.
I cannot live a good life if I'm living for everyone else.
*From this day on, I put **my** well-being first.*
I am worthy of love.
I look at myself in the mirror
and love everything about me.
I am the best version of myself right now.
I go forward bravely, whether afraid or unsure.
I choose peace.
I choose joy.
I choose me.

Release of Guilt & Shame

I release all energy of guilt.
I am not guilty.
I am perfectly me.
I release all energy of shame.
I am not ashamed.
I am proud that I'm a survivor.
I release all energy of self-judgment.
I am not on this earth to be judged.
My purpose is to live, experience life, grow and learn.
I embrace all my flaws with unconditional love.
My imperfections make me unique.
I embrace all my scars and invisible wounds.
They are not a karmic burden but, instead, reminders of
how strong I am.
I embrace all that I am, light and dark, positive and
negative, perfect and imperfect.
I am vulnerable with myself.
I am worthy of unconditional love.
I forgive all my flaws with compassion.
I love myself for all that I am!
I am fucking* awesome!
I AM!

*Fucking is optional.

Victim Blaming

The idea that abuse, neglect, or dysfunction that we've endured is somehow our responsibility or fault is ridiculous. I mean no offense to men, but the patriarchal societal model has played an enormous role in victim blaming. Fuck the patriarchy! Society doesn't want to take responsibility for the poisonous history of masculine, energy-driven abuses of the past that lives on today. Blaming the victim helps keep those in power and abuse of power in power! **VICTIMS ARE NOT TO BLAME!**

If our abuser has gaslit us so much that we believe we're dumb, always wrong, or incapable of this or that, it doesn't mean it's true. If people don't acknowledge our person as powerful, with rights and boundaries, that is also not our problem; that is their problem and they need to respect us or leave.

EXERCISE

- Do you remember who you really are?
- How far back do you have to go to remember your innocence? Your love of all things?
- When was the last time you had fun, without alcohol or recreational drugs?
- When was the last time you danced or sang and didn't care who was around to witness it? Have you ever?

None of us is to blame if we have been harmed by another person. By abusing their power, the perpetrator broke through our safety zone and overtook our power without consent. We are not to blame if someone has hurt us or accused us of making them hurt us. (That's gaslighting, by the way.) We do not have the power to overtake their free will and they do not have the right to take ours. We are worthy of that boundary; we are worthy of respect. Each of us has the power over our own destiny. Don't play the past on loop. Don't believe the lies someone told you either. You are worth more than they said.

It is so difficult to stand in our truth and power when we're in survival mode. In PTSD survival mode, we are only capable of REacting rather than ACTing, as in taking action, verbalizing boundaries, or asserting ourselves. Until we feel safe enough to sit with and dig in to the space and energy of the trauma, we can't feel safe, steady, or grounded enough to thrive, to really **live** life! That should not be anyone's reality! We are all capable of rising out of and breaking fee of toxic life patterns, even though it is not easy. Like a phoenix rising from the ashes, we can rebirth ourselves, stronger, balanced, safe, and the truest being that we've ever been.

When we can stand steady in our own power and truth for even a few minutes, doors and windows that have been sealed shut for years can open. That moment is beautiful! There is strength in the stillness. Like the eye of a storm, we can have a moment of peace and quiet and enjoy the absence of chaos. That clarity can help us get out of a bad situation or move forward into healing. In the stillness amidst the chaos, we can rediscover or realize our inner strength. The true self is present, waiting to emerge. We are resilient, no longer a victim and more than a survivor.

All healers are warriors. In order to heal, we must battle our shadows, abusers, and shame to save our lives and souls. It takes great courage to do this. We are warriors! It doesn't matter when that moment comes. We start when we're ready. We're choosing ourselves. That is all that matters.

I Embrace My Inner Warrior!

I embrace all that I am, light and dark.
I am not a victim;
I am a warrior!
I release, with compassion,
all emotions and pain of the past.
The past has been laid to rest.
I am free from hurt, abuse, and neglect.
I am free.
I am safe.
They (he/she) can no longer hurt me.
They (he/she) have no power over me.
I honor my needs and boundaries.
I am empowered!
I am strong.
I am steady and rooted to the earth
and protected on high!
I reconnect to my higher self.
I feel my inner courage replace any emotions
that ruled over me.
I am not a worrier;
I am a warrior!
I recognize my free will.
I am ready to step forward;
I am ready to leave behind the pile of ashes and rise up
like the phoenix
and begin the life I choose...
Right here. Right now.
I am all that I am!

Reclaiming Power

Soul retrieval is a term that Shamans use when referring to recapturing fractured energetic aspects of the soul that are related to trauma. It's as if we left part of our soul in the space and time of the traumatic event. It definitely may feel that way. When trauma happens, we are faced with our fight, flight, or freeze response. This is subconscious; we react in a primal and instinctive way. Whenever someone victim blames and says things like, "Why didn't you fight back? Why didn't you run?" it's as ridiculous as asking someone why they blink. Fight, flight, or freeze is not something we control; it's an involuntary defense or coping mechanism of our body. As we can see in nature, some animals freeze, some flee, and some fight. We are mammals that may do any of these and, depending on the circumstances, the response may vary.

When working with trauma in energy work, there is an energetic wound left in the body and in the timeline of when this event happened. Many clients need this kind of karmic trauma energy to be cleared and some "soul retrieval" work, which I prefer to refer to as "reclaiming your power."

In this process, there is a reunion of one part of a person with the part that feels "lost." It's not lost; we are never lost. There may be a fracture in our sense of self and our well-being. The traumatic event is written in each of our Akashic Records, or Book of Life. It may not have been part of our karma, but it becomes part of it as we learn to heal and overcome through the deep strength and divine power inside ourselves. It's like that crack in the bowl that needs to be repaired with liquid gold; except in my work, it's healed with light, love, and Reiki energy.

I often write an affirmation for a client when we've had a particularly challenging or eventful session and I want them to continue self-care afterward. When I had a few clients in a row who needed to affirm reclaiming their power, I realized that this special affirmation had to be shared. This was also the "Aha!" moment when I realized that these affirmations needed to be shared globally in the form of this book. If you also need to reclaim your power as we all journey forward in this uncertain world, may these words help you find your inner strength once again!

I Reclaim My Power

I now reclaim my power.
I stand steady in my body,
grounded to Earth,
connected to and protected by the heavens.
I release all energy that does not belong to me or serve my
highest good.
I call back and reclaim all my power:
From anyone who has taken it or held it,
From every corner of the earth,
From all the spirals of the cosmos.
I reclaim my power!
I stand strong.
I am empowered!
All that once felt undone or imbalanced is restored;
I am healed.
I am.

Chapter 8

The Heart Center

"Nothing we do, however virtuous, can be accomplished alone; therefore, we are saved by love."
– Reinhold Niebuhr

"Unconditional love really exists in each of us. It is a part of our deep inner being. It is not so much an active emotion as a state of being."
– Ram Dass

Heart Chakra

Oh, the heart chakra! (sigh) We know this one! It's called the Anahata chakra. Most of us have loved, been loved, had our heart broken, or grieved for someone. Human beings are born with a need for social connection, affection and the ability to love unconditionally, no judgment or hate, just trusting in the power of love. So many of us lose that along the way after growing up in a dysfunctional family. However, even if we have not been unconditionally loved, a nurturing parent or grandparent in childhood, many of us find love along the way in friendships or romance later on. People are social and we, generally, crave contact with others.

The Anahata chakra is key in emotional healing. If we don't love in a healthy way or we grew up with conditional rather than unconditional love, we feel broken, unloved, or unlovable. We often attract the love we think we deserve based on our past or childhood, even if it was neglectful or abusive. If you feel that way, please ask yourself why would you be put here on earth if you were unlovable? There are many creatures on this earth that are gross, slimy, or ugly, but there's always someone or some other slimy, ugly creature that loves it back! I promise that we are all loved and lovable!

Some of us are born into a family of chaos, violence, mental illness, addiction, or abuse. In these families, it is hard to feel loved. Please take a moment to consider this…

- What if you were born to help these lost souls find their way back to light and love?
- What if you're here not to perpetuate their abuse or anger to make others feel unloved, but instead, you're here to break the chain of abuse, so that you can heal your heart and the heart of every single soul in your ancestral line?

Unfortunately, one family member often feels like the black sheep or the punching bag for everyone else, that person who sees the broken or the abusive behavior and wants out. I encourage you to get out, because that will help you to heal yourself. It is nearly impossible to heal from the poison we've been eating, drinking, and breathing if we are still in the place where that poison is being served every single day. I do know some people who are actively working at it, but it takes a lot longer and, frankly, I don't know anyone who has done it fully and successfully yet. By getting out, we immediately set a boundary, a geographic one, which breaks the chains of abuse and can often change the course of history in our families.

Once I woke up to the reality of the dysfunction in my family, I put all my focus and manifestation energy on moving out. It was years of suicidal thoughts, fear, and tiptoeing around feelings in my family and practically taking a vow of silence so I would not wake the lion or bear. Yes, both of my parents had tempers. Both parents had had dysfunctional childhoods themselves, and I stand here today with great compassion for both of them and their journeys. However, at some point as an adult, I had to choose me and my life. I knew I mattered and I had a purpose, even if I hadn't figured it out yet. I definitely wasn't confident or courageous enough to pursue it.

Our heart knows what we need and craves it. Sometimes we are subconsciously drawn to the comfort of dysfunction, because we're used to it; but when we go deeper into the purest part of our soul, the safe space, we know we want and need unconditional love.

As we develop our energetic, spiritual being, our heart chakra expands into a fifth dimensional vibration and feelings become multidimensional. We begin to feel the collective, universal, unconditional love for all living beings, humanity, and the planet. We drop prejudices and judgment and begin to trust and feel the truth about our own and other people's hearts.

In the energetic sense of the body, there are three brains: the actual brain, the heart, and the gut. When we follow any of the guidance from these brains, we can make decisions, particularly if we don't let ego, the inner critic, or limiting beliefs have any say in the decision-making process. Remember, all wisdom passes through the heart for us to truly learn. When we make decisions with our heart, our choice is based on love.

The Wisdom of My Heart

All wisdom is filtered through the heart brain.
My heart beats.
My heart feels.
My heart is the force of my lifeblood.
*I **am** a force!*
I am powerful and important.
I embrace all of my strengths and weaknesses,
all of my missteps, mistakes, heartbreaks,
triumphs, and loves.
They are all gifts.
Feelings are a gift, a pathway to growth.
I feel because I am.
All wisdom is downloaded and translated
through the heart.
When I expose my heart, with vulnerability,
I allow for wisdom to become knowledge
in all aspects of my self.
I am connected to all other living beings.
We are one.
I am whole and I am part of a whole collective.
I am complete; we are complete and connected.
I am grateful for all of the connections of my past, present,
and future.
Thank you for all the lessons in love.
I am grateful and graciously accept and give back love.

"Almost all of you misunderstand what unconditional love is. It is holding vibrational alignment with who you are no matter what is going on around you."
– Abraham Hicks

Unconditional Love

Unconditional love is a term that's thrown around in casual conversation so often, perhaps it has lost its meaning. This kind of love is one without any limitations. There are no dangling carrots, terms, or conditions; this is pure and complete love. This love can be shared with a parent and child, siblings, family, friends, or a lover. The most important person with whom to share this love is ourselves. This is the one who gets forgotten so frequently.

Unconditional love means that someone loves us exactly as we are. The perfect unconditional love song is Billy Joel's "Just the Way You Are." No one should have to change to earn the love of another person. Unfortunately, so many of us try to mold ourselves to or change for another person in different ways. If we were raised in an unhealthy or dysfunctional family, we spend much of our adult lives chasing love, but instead usually attract the conditional kind that leaves us wanting more and feeling worse about ourselves.

When we love without questioning ourselves, our worthiness, or the other person, that is unconditional love. When someone loves and accepts all our perceived flaws and little imperfections, that is unconditional love. When someone recognizes our triggers and our issues and can be present for us through that, while helping us feel safe and loved, **that** is unconditional love! In order to find that, each of us has to dig in to our emotional past and find the areas that caused us to believe that we're unworthy of this kind of love. We must have trust, faith, and 100 percent belief that we are worthy, just as every human being is worthy of unconditional love. Now that statement doesn't mean that we have to like everyone. That is not our responsibility. However, even those we do not like deserve a little compassion. This book is for you, so let's start there.

Vulnerability

I release all emotional, mental, and karmic baggage
that no longer serves me.
I am safe in my body.
I am safe in my heart.
I am safe in this time and space.
It is safe to be vulnerable.
It is safe to love and be loved.
I am worthy of unconditional love.
I am worthy, safe, and free to love platonically
and passionately!
I am ready.

My heart beats.
My heart feels.
My heart is a well of life force.
My heart is the force behind my life blood.
I AM a force!
I am powerful and important.
I experience all emotions and feelings through my heart.
My heart is the brain through which all wisdom
becomes knowledge.
I learn through emotions, vulnerability, heartbreak,
pain, grief, and sorrow.
Feelings are a gift.
I accept these gifts and sit with my feelings.
I feel because I am.
I am connected to all living beings;
I am never alone, yet, by myself, I am whole.
The deepest spark of divine life force is at the core of
my body, mind, and soul.
I am safe when I am vulnerable; I am loved.

Let That Shit Go!

Sometimes, without even realizing it, we hold on to baggage (emotional or mental) without even realizing it. From a young age, we're told to "forgive and forget," and think if we say "I forgive you," that all is right with the world. Just to say the words is not always enough. We may say it, even to ourselves, but we still store the feelings related to an incident or a person somewhere in our mind and body. We sometimes play an event over and over again in our heads, not really forgiving anything at all. Everyone else might have let it go and we continue to criticize ourselves over and over and over again. That kind of repetitive energy often gets stuck somewhere in our body as well as our mind. Even if we forget about it after time, the feelings may still lie dormant in our bodies and creep up on us in a new way, like pain or tension.

Here's where Reiki comes in handy. Reiki helps move energy and raise our energetic frequency. We all start life in an energetically perfect and aligned in body and spirit. Then life throws experiences at us that push us out of alignment. Reiki is the divine light or pure energy we started with as a soul that keeps us alive. In a Reiki healing session, the energy of the universe flows through us to clear away what we're ready to clear and that which no longer serves our greatest good.

Once I had a mother come for Reiki with her baby and the baby wanted in on receiving. She stretched out her arms at times and stared into my eyes at other moments. Then she telepathically told me that Reiki felt like heaven—the warmth, the tingling, the almost musical vibration it brings was reminding her of her time before birth. My eyes were opened by this young-bodied old soul, schooling me on Reiki and heaven. We all have the potential to live and love in that vibration, with a little release and optimism.

A little tangent: Letting baggage go doesn't mean you stuff it down or ignore it. It also doesn't mean you pretend that thing never happened. That doesn't help us spiritually grow. Instead, it keeps us stuck in a closed loop of inviting the same pain until we wake up and say, "Enough!"

Sometimes pain, illness, or negative feelings can help us move forward on our spiritual path. Anger or resentment can help push us through a difficult task just to prove to ourselves that we are capable of doing something no one else believed we could. Sometimes negative people serve as a mirror or motivator to change something out of alignment, pushing us to rise up to our greater potential.

At times, in a session, a client or I (or both of us) hear a voice saying "Let go!" Often, it's repeated, and the client will relax and let go. Suddenly, a flow or burst of energy will move through the person and I will notice their breath change; their body becomes more balanced and relaxed. They may even fall asleep.

We are not always ready to "let go" and release negative energy, pain, or illness, even if it no longer serves a purpose. Subconsciously, we don't even realize it's there. We hold on to it to mull over or we've just grown comfortable with it, and fear of the unknown encourages us to keep it.

In a Reiki session, when we resist releasing the bad stuff, a Reiki practitioner cannot make us let go; no one can. Everything comes back to our own personal power and free will. A practitioner can continue to let Reiki flow and allow for the greatest amount of energy a person is willing to receive (consciously and subconsciously).

So how can we get out of our own way and "let it go"? On a conscious level, it can be very difficult. The "forgive and forget" method doesn't work, because it encourages us to forget, and we can't. It's better to actually dig in to and sit with the feelings of the hurt, wrongdoing, or self-judgment so that the pain no longer hurts us over and over again. We have to ask ourselves why we feel this way and what's really going on. If we don't explore it and work through it, the pain, hurt, tension, anger, or shame will keep coming back.

Reiki can help open us up and clear what we're willing to release. Then it's important to continue on our own self-healing journey. It can be as simple as replacing a negative thought with a positive one (affirmations), exercising, or meditating. Some of my clients do a combination of yoga and Reiki or Reiki and therapy. Some clients go to therapy for years before starting working with me and are able to see progress after only a few Reiki sessions through opening and clearing buried issues. It's important to have outlets

outlets to let it go in a healthy way so that we don't allow our feelings and hurtful thoughts to get stuck. It's a beautiful thing to find inner balance and peace. Whatever we're struggling with, perhaps it's time to let it go with the help of a therapist, life coach, or Reiki Master.

Emotional Baggage

With love and forgiveness,
I release all emotional baggage that no longer serves me.
With love and forgiveness,
I release all negative thought patterns and limiting beliefs.
I let go of the burdens of other people's baggage.
I free myself from all energy of self-doubt, self-criticism,
and self-destruction.
I feel my feet and my seat firmly planted
and grounded to the earth,
like the roots of a tree, reaching deeper and deeper
into the earth.
I am steady.
I trust myself.
I trust in the earth and the universe that I am safe.
I know that I am loved.
I love myself.
I love myself at all ages, in all moods.
I love all facets and qualities that make me me.
When I express self-care and self-love,
I empower others to love themselves and attract more
unconditional love into our lives and into the world.
I am ready to live my own destiny by my own free will!
I carry only my own karma.
I am fulfilling my karmic destiny!
I am evolving.
I am healing.
I AM.

Meditation on Ancestral Love

Breathe...
    Inhale...
    Exhale...
    Feel the breath going all the way down to the bottom of your
lungs.
    Exhale completely, as if you are squeezing out a sponge.
    Breathe into the bottom of your lungs. Be brave and breathe
into the spaces of all your heartbreak.
    Breathe out and allow yourself to feel those feelings...
You are safe...no one can hurt you now. These are just feelings.
    See yourself at whatever age you were then. Go back to any
time, age, or event in your life that needs healing now. Whatever
moment that comes up, stay with it. Keep breathing.
    Who is the person who hurt you or broke your heart? What
do you wish they would have done differently? What does that look
like?
[PAUSE]
    What would you do differently with the knowledge that you
have now? Can you imagine that now? If you cannot, imagine your
present self, stepping into that scene and protecting you at that
younger age. Tell the other person to step back and stop hurting
younger you. Breathe in and out. Keep breathing.   You are safe.
Embrace your younger self. Can you do it? Can you see it?
    Breathe…
    Cry if you need to cry. Let go of the pain, the fear, and the
anger...let it all go. Breathe in love. You are worthy! You are so
worthy of love! Keep breathing.
[PAUSE]
    Do you feel love for your younger self? Can you feel the
loving embrace with your past self?
    You are enough.
    You are lovable.
    You are important.
    Feel the hug.
    Feel the love.

Feel the apology to yourself for holding on to this pain, shame, and guilt. It's time to let it go and reclaim your childhood, your inner child.

Feel the forgiveness from the younger you. Younger you is proud of present you. Sit with that feeling. You made it! You survived! You are okay. In this safe space, say anything else you need to, and listen, with your heart, to your younger self. Shout, scream, and cry together if you need to. Let everything go. Breathe...

[PAUSE]

Stay for just a little bit longer, but it's just about time to come back to now. Thank younger you for being so strong and brave back then. Thank yourself for allowing the feelings and memories to come up to release and transmute from fear, heartbreak, or pain into unconditional love.

Now breathe in.

Breathe out and say: *I am lovable.*

Breathe in...you are so worthy of love.

And breathe out and say: *I am loved.*

You are loved...even if, right now, just for now, you believe that love only comes from your cat. You are so loved. You are now attracting more love, unconditional love.

Breathe in and put your hands on your heart.

Breathe out:

I am love.

I am loved.

I am lovable.

I AM.

Let everything else go...let it all go. Tap your feet together. Wiggle your fingers and toes. Give yourself a hug now. Tap your arms in this hug.

You are loved.

You are steady and grounded.

You are healing.

You are safe.

Inner Child & Karma Work

Most times, if we're not attracting unconditional love, we have to look at our parents' relationship as well as our relationship with them. This is not about blame, no matter what your family modeled for you. As adults, we all must take responsibility for ourselves and our actions or inactions. Life is a journey and series of experiences and experiments to find ourselves, our truest selves, and improve and expand on our depth and our soul's potential. To reach our soul's goals, it may not be an easy stroll down a flat path. It's more likely a winding, hilly, rocky path that we have to walk.

Spiritually, we choose our parents well before we are even a thought in our grandparents' minds. (Remember from Chapter 5, you were an egg in your mother's ovaries when she was growing in your grandmother's womb.) Whenever the concept of choosing our parents comes up, people say, "Why on earth would I pick them?" There's not always an easy answer there, but choosing them as our parents may not always be to have amazing, loving parents; that may be too easy. In some scenarios, we choose a challenging life to become the best possible version of ourselves. We may choose to be the child to help our parents become better people. Sometimes it works out and sometimes it doesn't.

Again, there is no blame with this life model. We need to love ourselves unconditionally and embrace all of our good and bad qualities. We each arrived on earth, usually, as perfect as we possibly could be. If you're open-minded to past lives, how we left earth after the last lifetime may affect this life's tasks or obstacles, but we are always born practically perfect. It's almost as if we pick up where we left off, but in a new body, place, and situation, with amnesia, of course! We often return with some of the same soul family, also in different bodies and roles.

Think about the people we work with in our careers. There are people we always love to be on projects with. This is the same concept, but in various lives. Each of us needs the help of this amazing team, so that we can grow and evolve each lifetime. There's a chance one of us may be the team leader of many of the weakest members of former teams. Whatever role we've picked, we have chosen a very worthy task of teaching and leading others, as well as learning from them. We are all here to support one another with understanding and compassion and to help every one of us become wiser, stronger, more confident, more loving, and on and on. Most of us will not become this self-aware, but some of us will awaken to quite a bit of our purpose when we begin to feel our calling or follow our deep, burning desire and destiny.

If we choose parents who are not the greatest parents for us, that's okay. Trust that there are lessons to be learned from these family members. However, if we buy in to conditional love, blame, abuse, or neglect and play that out by treating ourselves with the same disregard and disrespect as our elders, we cannot attract unconditional love. We, instead, will only attract the same abuse, neglect, and negativity.

Consider that there is no perfect childhood. Our parents may have had a dysfunctional, neglectful, or abusive upbringing. Their parents may have. It's a cycle and most people reading this book are the chain breakers of the family who have the opportunity to prevent future cycles of dysfunction, abuse, or trauma. We may choose our parents for the early lessons, but if it feels like they failed us as a child and continue failing us as an adult, they may no longer serve our highest good. They may no longer be the teachers we need. We must set boundaries and intentions to create our new tribe now!

Manifest the new chosen family that will call us out on our own bullshit and hold us accountable so that we may rise up to be the best possible version of ourselves! It's time to love and nurture ourselves the way we need, and to parent and nurture our own children to break the cycle. This is how we heal the past, present, and future all at once.

Freedom from the Past

I send unconditional love to all anger and sadness.
I release the pain.
I forgive everything.
I cut the cords and break the chains that hold me to
patterns of abuse, neglect, judgment, and unworthiness.
I release you.
I send back all energetic cords that do not belong to me or
serve my life's purpose.
You no longer have any power over me.
I am my own power source.
I am my own advocate.
I am free!

Meditation on Healing the Mother Wound

Find a comfortable place to sit. A chair, a sofa, the floor, or wherever you want. You can even lie down for this. If you're reading this, I will give you cues to take a pause and go into your mind's eye. Take your time.

Close your eyes and take a deep breath all the way down to your belly, filling your lungs completely. Breathe out and let go of all the air in your lungs. Repeat this breath three times.

Breathe in down to your navel. Breathe out slow and easy.

Breathe in, bringing all your attention to the navel. You can even put your hands on your belly there. Breathe out. Feel how your belly moves as you breathe in and out. Feel your body heavy on the chair, floor, bed, or sofa. You are safe.

Tune in to the navel. Allow your mind to travel back in time when your navel was connected to an umbilical cord and you were inside your mother's womb. Tiny, warm, cozy, safe, and loved. No matter your relationship with your birth mother, at this moment in history, your mother's soul loved your soul and your mother's body loved, nurtured and nourished your growing body inside hers. Your cells intermingled. Many of your cells live inside her and hers live inside you for the rest of your lives. You are forever bonded in body and soul. For that, she knows you and connects with you in a way that no other human being can.

Breathe...

In and out.

You might see a glow of pink light around the round, cozy space where you are growing. You are safe in the womb. Stay there for a little while and feel the warm energy of life force flowing into your body, through the umbilical cord, cellularly, energetically, lovingly. You are loved. You are wanted. Even if you are to be adopted, you are wanted by both of your families. You are wanted in this world. You are safe. You are enough. You are safe in your mind. You are safe in the womb. You are in the safest space that exists in the world. Just be with these sensations and see what comes up for you.

[PAUSE]

Now imagine that this umbilical cord is magical. It is glowing with light. Follow the curves and spirals of your umbilical cord and allow it to magically travel back to your mother in your grandmother's womb. You are a microscopic egg in your mother's developing ovaries. The three of you are connected. You are safe in your mother's developing body; she is safe, developing in her mother's womb. She is loved. You are loved. You are both being nurtured. You are both perfect at this moment in the past.
[PAUSE]

Allow any feelings to rise up that need to. You are safe. Breathe. Keep breathing.

You and your mother have chosen this path and this family long before. Travel back, once again, through the umbilical cord of time and go to your great-grandmother's womb with your grandmother as a developing fetus. Your mother, an egg in your grandmother's developing ovaries. This karmic connection, this karmic contract, was written before any of these women were born. All of you chose to be in this world together, to be related in this way. This is your soul's karmic contract: To help each other evolve, improve, and grow. You were just a soul at that point. Watching over this connection. Observing your future family. For better or for worse, you are all connected spiritually and physically in this life.

Take a brief **PAUSE** and consider that. Allow any feelings to arise and sit with them. Cry or laugh if you feel moved to.

Take in the wisdom and knowledge that when your mother was in your grandmother's womb, you already had picked which egg would become you. And when fertilization was about to happen, or perhaps before, you chose the sperm that would make you exactly the person you wanted to be. You only allowed that one sperm entry into the egg. You chose your father too. You could see the image of your future self with each permutation. You predicted your eye color, your hair color and texture, your height, your genetic challenges, and your genetic strengths. You knew exactly what you needed in this life and set it up for the best possible scenario and outcome. You were perfect. You are perfectly you now.

Keep breathing and take this time and space to explore that time, those feelings, and whatever you need to find balance. Breathe.

[PAUSE]

Now take a deep breath in and out. Feel yourself traveling forward in time through the spirals and curves of the magical umbilical cord, filled with great, healing light. As you time-travel to the present, feel the love once more. Feel yourself being born again, surrounded by love. You are loved. You are so loved. Your family chose you and you chose them. If you are in an adoptive or dysfunctional family, there was love to bring you forward into this world and get you to the family you're in now, especially your chosen family of like-minded people. Some paths are more complicated than others. You are on the right path for you.

Breathe deeply into your belly and feel your belly rise and expand. You are back in the present moment. Breathe out. You are safe in your body. You are exactly where and when you are supposed to be. Feel your presence. Feel the space you take up. Feel your importance in this world. You are wanted. You are needed. You are worthy. You are enough.

Wiggle your fingers and toes. Tap your feet together. Clap your hands three times. Gently blink your eyes.

May you go forward, from now on, with great purpose, knowing how valuable and valued your life is. Namaste. Have a wonderful day!

Daddy Issues

We can't address mother issues without addressing father issues. So many of us have absent, emotionally unavailable, or downright abusive fathers. No one has the right to abuse us. Our parents, ideally, are emotionally available, supportive to helping us become our best selves and to catch us when we fall or aren't perfect. I do know a few people who grew up in that environment, but many of us didn't. How do we overcome that absence or abuse? It's not a simple answer.

The Ho'oponono (coming up later in the chapter) is a wonderful tool for healing a lot of parent wounds. It's an effective way to come at the emotions with compassion for everyone. Our parents are not perfect. No human being had a perfect childhood. This is part of the educational journey of life. When we recognize our parents' painful childhoods, we can find the sympathy and begin healing ourselves and, potentially, the wounded relationships with them.

Energetically, mothers are the nurturer and model for emotions and caring. Fathers energetically represent our self-confidence. How do we see ourselves in the world? When the father figure is absent in our lives, we may constantly question our self-worth throughout life. Note that I wrote "father figure." We don't need a dad to learn how to navigate the world, but it helps to have a father figure, no matter the gender or title.

When it comes time to have relationships, friends, or lovers, we begin to play out a lot of the scenarios that were modeled in childhood. It is helpful to clear away anything that doesn't serve our highest good or our potential partner's.

Farewell to the Father Heartache

*Dad, I acknowledge you and I thank you for your part
in bringing me into this world.
Without you, I would not exist.
I thank you for any and all traits and gifts
I have received from you.
I release all expectations;
you are you and I am me.*

*I apologize for any ways that
I contributed to our fractured relationship.
I forgive you for any ways you hurt me.
I let go of any expectations
for how I hoped our relationship could be.
I let it all go with the past.
You are you and I am me.*

*I wish you peace.
I grant your pardon in my heart.
I release all emotional, physical, and mental pain
with this pardon.
You no longer hold power over me or my feelings.
I choose happiness, confidence, and unconditional love
from now on.
You are you and I am me.
I am perfectly me.*

Forgiveness

There are many misconceptions attached to forgiveness. We can forgive someone or an action and still have every right to not allow a person or action back into our lives. Some people are serial abusers and serial apologizers; that doesn't mean we accept those attack actions against us. That is not forgiveness. Forgiveness is letting go of the shame, guilt, anger, and pain attached to the action(s) or incident being forgiven. If there is no remorse on the other side, part of forgiveness is letting go of that person. This is part of self-care, self-preservation, and self-love.

When we love and value ourselves, we say "Yes!" to what we need to thrive and "No!" to what causes us pain and harm. Let's keep the body temple and energy field clear and forgive, especially ourselves for anything we feel unworthy of or guilty about. We all deserve peace!

For years, I found forgiveness challenging. For the simplest wrongdoings, sure, I was fine, but for big trauma or mistreatment, I found the word alone was a trigger. Forgive. "You must forgive. It is a gift to yourself." In the realm of trauma, neglect, abandonment, or abuse, it felt like giving that person a pass or pardon.

No person ever explained it to me in a way that I could accept forgiving the worst of mistreatments or injustices. And no human being ever showed me the proper way to forgive. It was my work with the angels and the Akashic Records that showed me the depth of karma and how damaging the energy of unforgiven really is to ourselves.

Forgiveness is more about replacing resentment and hurt with love, compassion, and unconditional self-love. If we don't fill those formerly knotted and hurt spaces with positive loving kindness, the negative energy festers and can manifest into illness, self-harm, or even self-loathing. Forgiveness lightens our emotional, mental, and spiritual load. The baggage we carry of guilt, shame, anger, fear, or resentment is quite heavy.

As I mentioned earlier, I receive messages from the spirit world during sessions. In one Reiki session, a new way of understanding forgiveness was explained to me. When someone harms us or hurts our feelings, we have to feel those feelings. It may take time to work through that, but we can't fully heal until we forgive at a deep spiritual level. The pace is really up to our comfort level. Somewhere down the line, in the healing process, when we think about the situation or the person, we are triggered and brought right back to that pain, guilt, shame, or anger from the past. This is trauma. Trauma is basically reliving the moment in time, over and over again. They are out living their life! And we are left with this bag of hurt!

Toni Morrison said, "You wanna fly, you got to give up that shit that weighs you down."

The person or people who harmed us have forgotten about the wrongdoing or possibly completely forgotten about us and we are carrying stinky old baggage that they left with us. At some point, we have to say, "Why am I still carrying around the responsibility for this pain?!" That baggage is not for us to carry. It was karmically never meant to be ours. The event became part of our life experience and we were given an opportunity to find our strength, the divine power inside ourselves, to rise up and overcome it.

Never think that anything bad that happens is a punishment. If something happens against our will, someone else's fear, anger, and free will was imposed on us, and we do not have to carry around their offensive, heavy attack as our burden. Though we did not deserve whatever that event or situation was that caused us such enduring anguish in our souls, it is our responsibility to overcome and continue on to be the best version of ourselves that we can be. We can heal. We don't have to forget. Forget is not part of forgiveness. We cannot fully heal until we unpack the feelings and let go of the baggage that the other person left us with.

If you get nothing else out of this book, may you gain the true power of forgiveness through this! Forgiveness, in my opinion, is truly the greatest gift we can give ourselves and the key to all healing—by letting go of the pain a person or event left us feeling. There is no gift or value in carrying around pain, anger, or shame for a lifetime. That is not a life. That is not our purpose in this lifetime! If you want to come back and do it over again, by all means, keep carrying the rotting bag or bags with you. It's only a matter of time before the bottom rots out and we will have to deal with it in crisis. But instead, if we want to take our power back and start living our best life, forgive. Make the choice and say, "I choose me! I love myself too much to walk around with this pain, anger, and shame anymore!" Drop what's hurting you. Let it go. Let it all go.

We are worthy of unconditional love. We deserve peace and harmony. May this affirmation help inspire or continue the release of pain and the embrace of strength, value, and confidence. We each have autonomy and purpose. We are free!

I Am Free

I send unconditional love
to all anger and sadness within me.
I release the pain.
I let it all go.
I choose life.
I embrace peace.
You can no longer hurt me.
I let it all go.
I forgive everything
that depletes me and holds me back.
I am healing.
I am free!

The Ho'oponono

The Ho'oponono is a traditional ancient Hawaiian practice of restoring balance, forgiveness and reconciliation. The practice of Ho'oponono is used by indigenous healers all through the region of the South Pacific, beyond Hawaii and into Tahiti and as far as New Zealand. It is beginning to make its way to the West now, as it's a powerful and effective way to heal family wounds. It was specifically used to repair broken relationships within a family, providing freedom from the past. If there is anger, guilt, or stress, the body is weak and vulnerable to illness. It's vital to keep the vibration within a family whole and together.

There are entire courses to learn about the process and traditional values of Ho'oponono. It is not my place or calling to teach that to anyone here. However, the Ho'oponono begins with a beautiful expression of taking responsibility for any action or words that contributed to the misunderstanding or rift that happened in the family. It is the most beautiful expression of humanity and grace, including an apology, asking forgiveness, giving gratitude, and expressing love. So I had to share it in this book. Please know, I share this with love and honor to the Hawaiian community and culture.

I'm sorry.
Please forgive me.
Thank you.
I love you.

I recognize the power of affirmations and this Hawaiian one is extremely effective. It works for people in recovery. Taking ownership of our role in relationship problems is key to healing ourselves as well as our relationships with others, past, present, or future. With this type of practice, we are sharing love and harmonizing with others as a collective: one people.

I began to see how easily this practice could work for a variety of issues and situations. My alternate version for separating

from a toxic person or releasing a traumatic situation:
I forgive you.
I release you.
I love you.
Thank you.

With love, acknowledgement, and respect, I offer an "extended remix" version of Ho'oponono. It's a way of showing that the short version can be adapted in any way we need to forgive or apologize, restoring balance and harmony for the greatest good.

I'm sorry...
>*for the resentment and anger I feel for you.*

Please forgive me...
>*for that negative energy.*

I forgive you...
>*for all the ways I feel you failed me and for not loving me more or the way I expected.*

I love you...*regardless.*
>*I thank you for the lessons I learned from you.*
>*I let go of all the pain and hurt I've been holding all these years.*
>*I let it go with love.*
>*I let it go with love.*
>*I let it go with love...back to the universe, where it may be transmuted into positive energy.*
>*I am grateful for all that I am and the potential I have to be even better.*

I thank you...
>*for helping me see myself and my self-worth.*
>*I embrace all that I am.*
>*I am worthy of love.*
>*I am loved.*
>*I am love.*
>*I AM!*

Grief

For many of us, holidays, birthdays, and anniversaries can be a big trigger for grief. Sometimes smells, songs, and meals can bring on waves of melancholy or grief as well. I am not immune.

People often call me when a family member or friend is terminally ill and getting ready to pass on. I do remote Reiki sessions for soul transition. I won't go into personal details, but it was time for one of my elderly clients to let go of her painful and sick body. She had lived a long life. She was a beautiful woman and had a big soul. As I linked with her energy field as she was leaving her body, she let me know that she was no longer in pain and she saw her husband waiting for her. She was at peace and ready. I felt her soul softly drifting away from her body.

With all I know about the afterlife, I still grieve for those who leave us, because love is our bond with one another. Grief is a symbol of our love. It is the love we still feel, but can no longer share in a physical way. It takes us time and practice to allow ourselves to feel that grief-love in a less painful way...and even when we think we're okay, a holiday, birthday, or anniversary comes and we're a weepy mess. It's okay to grieve; it's healthy, cleansing, and healing. Feel those emotions. Let it be, then let it go.

Grief is tricky. Our love for a person never dies or leaves us, so the feelings of grief can come up here and there for the rest of our lives.

A few years after my nana died, I saw rice pudding in the store. I never ate it, but she made it at every holiday...and somehow that triggered me to tears. I don't get that way anymore, but my kids think it's funny and tease me about it sometimes: "Rice pudding, Mom! Wah!" I can find the humor in it. That said, the reality is, we can't prepare for those moments—anything can trigger grief and sadness as if we just lost that person. Take comfort in knowing that our love endures, energy never dies, and our loved ones live on in spirit and feel that love for and from us.

When someone dies, time doesn't heal all wounds, but instead, it appears to not move in a straight line anymore. Honestly, it never did move straight ahead. It's something we humans created in calendars and clocks to show the passing of time. Time is not linear; it moves differently when we lose a loved one. We relive little moments from the past as if they are happening right now, because that is how soul-time works. The past and present touch together in our hearts and our memories. We need to allow ourselves to grieve for as long as we need. The more we love someone, the longer we may grieve. I am thankful for all the love in my life. Also, as sad or angry as I am over the losses, I continue to feel that love for and from them in their afterlife. They are never forgotten. They are not gone forever—just gone in this form. I am so grateful for Reiki and meditation and the ability to feel connected to them and ease grief in this way.

Any time we are grieving or others are grieving around us, we must be patient and hold a space for grief. Cry. Laugh. Smile. Ugly cry some more. And know we're not alone.

I Acknowledge My Grief

Today, I acknowledge loss.
I mourn.
I grieve.
I ache.
I suffer.
My heart hurts with absence.
I hold a space for this pain today, as a reminder
of how much I love you.
I apologize for any shortcomings or failures.
I forgive all.
Thank you for all the time, love,
experiences, and memories.
The memories and love live on
in my mind and my heart.
I look forward to the day that I feel your energy
with me again.
I invite you to visit my dreams.
May we heal all that needs to be healed between us.
Thank you for letting me in to your world
And being a part of mine.
I am who I am because you were in my life.
I regret nothing.
I miss you.
I love you.
I love me.
I send you unconditional love.
We are eternally connected.
Rest easy and so will I.
Namaste.

Death/Rebirth

Whether we are going through major life changes, or literally dying, we must go through the difficult and slow release of what I like to call "Shedding the Ego Stuff." According to what I have been shown and channeled in my work with people and souls crossing over, when we die, we go through a phase of shedding all the egocentric bullshit that doesn't matter in the afterlife. Anger, fear, judgment, and shame are just a few of the things that we shed when we get there. I believe that, initially, there may be some residue of grief as we miss our loved ones we've left behind. If our body was very sick, there may be energetic residue of that as we cross over. We spend time looking over our lives, past and future, and assess if we met the goals we hoped to and consider if we want to try again in another life. It may be a quick process or it might take a little longer, but, generally, we all go through it for as long as it takes to drop the ego.

  The same process happens here on earth in an incarnate life (As above, so below). When we close a chapter in our lives, like a breakup with a romantic partner or even a friend, we go through a grieving process. We reflect on the positive and negative aspects of the relationship, signs we missed, anything we want to avoid or do better next time. Ideally, if we give ourselves enough time being alone with our shadows and scars, we heal old wounds and we begin to love and respect ourselves unconditionally, and then will attract that kind of love and respect back. It's a rebirth of ourselves. We are ready for the next chapter in life. This time, we will attract better, because we know we are worthy and we recognize the signs and the booby traps to avoid.

Meditation on Shedding the Old

Find a comfortable and quiet place to sit or lie down and visualize. The room can be light or dark. Close your eyes and be aware of the light and dark behind your eyelids.

Breathe in deeply for a count of eight. Hold for four. Breathe out for a count of eight. Hold out for four. Do that a few times; edit the count to six or four if eight is too long.

Begin to put the focus back on the light and dark behind your eyelids. Relax the eyes. With your eyes gently closed, let your gaze "look" up, down, and side to side. Invite your third eye to open while your physical eyes stay closed.

See yourself before a mountain. It is a beautiful and colorful mountain with peaceful vibrations. Looking up, you can see only clouds, not the top of the mountain. Begin to climb. You walk or climb the path; a swift breeze blows by and you suddenly feel lighter. Your muscles are relaxed and you don't feel so heavy or weighed down on this journey. The wind has relieved you of your physical baggage. Let it go. Keep going.

As you climb, you find a depression in the mountain where there is a waterfall and a spring. You can use a drink, so you stop. You approach it and take a sip and you feel called to take a dip. Dressed, or any level of undress you prefer, you go into the spring; the water welcomes you. The spring is warm and glowing with light, reflecting all colors on its surface. Under the waterfall, you feel all your emotional baggage being washed away. Letting everything go, you feel a wave of peace and tranquility come over you, followed by a quick snap of urgency.

It's time to continue on your journey. As you continue your climb, you feel lighter. Though the path is getting steeper, you feel capable of almost anything, unless you are hearing the inner critic tell you "No you can't!" Gently ask them to settle down. "Yes, I can."

You see a sparkle reflected from a crevice in the rocks on the side of the path. You begin to dig into the earth carefully and feel something dense. You carefully dig around this object to find it is a crystal. You hold it in your hands and pull it in toward you and feel the inner critic leave. Imagine that your inner critic has traded places with the crystal and is now on the side of the path, to be neutralized by the earth.

You smile as you hold the crystal gently in your hands. You are proud of yourself for finding it, but you also feel the incredible vibrations coming from the crystal. You feel your mind expanding and the clouds are just out of your reach, glowing pink, blue, purple, and green. You feel as if you are floating and you feel yourself rise through the clouds to the top of the mountain. As you arrive at the top, you see loved ones who have passed, spirit guides, guardian angels, all there for you. They helped you uncover your own free will and power to rise to this level. You are ready to release your karmic baggage.

There is a large bonfire of red, orange, and yellow, pink, blue, purple, and even green. You sit in a circle with all the others who have been watching over you for many years or even lifetimes. You join hands with them and begin to see, feel, or hear the obstacles, the fights, the limiting beliefs, the life events that you need to let go. It's time.

Anything that no longer serves you begins to pour out of your body, mind, and soul and merge with the fire, where it is transformed into warm, loving energy. You may cry. You may make sounds as you release. Some of this may be difficult to release. You are safe with all of your spirit guides and guardians. The past can no longer harm you. Allow yourself to be free.

[PAUSE]

When you are ready, say the following out loud:

I release the past with gratitude;
I am thankful for all my past lessons,
triumphs, missteps, falters, and even
suffering.
I am all that I am.
I embrace all that I am, light and dark.
I am perfectly me.

Once you have completed this process, your guides surround you with a big group hug. You feel loved. You feel safe. You are loved and safe. They fill in any empty spaces within you with nurturing, healing energy. They repair your energy field and aura to full strength. You are so safe. You are worthy of unconditional love. You feel recharged and you know it's time to leave this beautiful place for now.

Take a deep breath in. As you exhale, it's as if you are floating down through the clouds.

Breathing in and out, nice and easy, your feet begin to gently touch the path. The farther you go down the mountainside, the heavier your feet are, feeling the force of gravity holding you in place, keeping you steady and grounded. Your feet are supported by the earth. Your mind is open to all possibilities. You are connected to the earth and the heavens.

As you get to the bottom of the mountain, you feel balanced. You are energized and relaxed. Breathe and begin to feel the weight of your body, supported by the earth, by the forces of gravity.
[PAUSE]

Repeat the following:

> *I am steady and safe.*
> *I am enough.*
> *I am perfectly me.*
> *I embrace all that I am.*
> *I am all that I am.*

Give yourself a hug. Pat your arms in an alternate pattern. Wiggle your fingers and toes and blink your eyes a bit before you go back to your day. Namaste!

Being Liked

We don't have to like or be liked by everyone. Not everyone will like or love us, because they are not at the same vibration as us or their vibration doesn't fit with ours. Think of music. When a whole orchestra is playing together, there are different instruments playing different notes at the same time that sound incredible all at once. Not every orchestral instrument fits in with all genres of music. We play different roles and march to our own rhythm and music. We are all different, yet part of the same collective humanity. We don't all like the same types of music and not everyone likes everyone else. It's important that we like ourselves and embrace our differences. I always say, "Embrace your weird!" That's what makes us interesting.

Whatever makes us different is often the most interesting quality we show the world. When we focus on what we don't like and reject an aspect of ourselves, we usually draw more negative attention to those things. When we're self-conscious about and put so much energy into the embarrassment or shame about that trait, we attract that same response. When we embrace the weird, we will attract people who see our differences as special, interesting, and lovable. We have to love all of ourselves if we want someone else to love us completely and unconditionally.

Your Theme Music

- Consider what your theme music would be.
  - Would it be silly or scary?
  - Would it be a serious march or a passionate waltz?
  - Would it sound romantic and flowery or dark and angry? Sit with this for a few minutes.
  - What songs are you drawn to most?
- How would people who love you describe you?
  - What words fit exactly who you are?
  - Is there a song that fits that description?
- Now consider the people who, for some unknown reason, don't like you.
- What kind of song do you think they would have following them through a movie?
- Does your song fit with theirs?

Even if people seem to be perfect matches for us as a friend or romantic partner, there's a possibility that they don't like themselves and we remind them of everything they dislike about themselves, or we remind them of their mother or father or someone they have baggage with. They may even treat us like they have baggage with us, though they don't know us well enough to actually have an issue with us at all. That's okay! We don't have to be liked by everyone! We attract what we need and what we put out into the world. If we are rejected, not liked, or ignored by someone, that person may not be meant to stay in our lives. They may have a purpose of bringing awareness to something about ourselves or some shadow we need to look at, and then they leave. We must stand in the vibration of grace and gratitude about all of our own traits, and even our past, so that negative people can be moved out of our path and we can continue to move forward with ease and flow.

There will be lots of opportunities to make friends and find or create a great tribe. There will be conflicts along the way too, because, though it may feel bad at the moment, it is our greatest good to learn some lessons from that person or from the conflict itself. Often, they are the mirror for our shadow and an important catalyst for growth.

I Open My Heart

*I open my heart to attract and receive acceptance
in all forms of unconditional love.
I fully accept myself, inside and out, light and dark,
positive and negative.
I embrace my weird with unconditional self-love.
I am who I am, right now.
I accept all that I am.
I attract others like me.
I welcome others to serve as a mirror to me, to help me
grow, evolve, and improve.
I let go of anyone in my life who does not accept me.
I release, with love, all who attempt to overpower,
direct, or poison my light soul.
I bravely choose to shine light on all of me.
I choose to sparkle!
I am me!
I am worthy.
I am enough.
I am awesome!*

Attraction

To attract caring friends and relationships, we must heal ourselves. There is no shortcut; it's work that each of us has to do. Life in our skin suits is all about mirrors and magnets. We attract what we put out in the world and what we need to see about ourselves, as well as opportunities to love and grow for the greater good and our personal greatest good. It's important that we take a little inventory of our current relationships when life feels challenging, including friends, family (parents and siblings are most important), and even coworkers and our bosses. Write down your responses right here or on a separate notepad.

What words would your friends use to describe you?

What words would your parents use to describe you?

How would your coworkers describe you?

How would your boss describe you?

What are the first three words that come to mind when you're describing yourself?

Are those words nice?

Do you believe them?

This exercise can be a challenge. Don't write them down, but consider how many negative words popped into your head as you struggled to write down positive ones. It is human conditioning to criticize rather than compliment. We have been programmed by modern society to be humble, when really, we are belittling ourselves. Confidence is not a negative quality. It is vital to our well-being. When we hold a bigger space to believe the negative things, those thoughts become manifested into who we believe we are. When we hold a space, allowing ourselves to be imperfect, but also recognizing our worth, our talents and our greatness, the world sees that. When we are confident at the tasks we do at work or in life, other people recognize our worth too. Believe the hype! Believe in yourself and live up to your greatness.

Chapter 9

Thymus Chakra & Health

"Do not believe in anything simply because you have heard it. Do not believe in anything simply because it is spoken and rumored by many. Do not believe in anything simply because it is found written in your religious books. Do not believe in anything merely on the authority of your teachers and elders. Do not believe in traditions because they have been handed down for many generations. But after observation and analysis, when you find that anything agrees with reason and is conducive to the good and benefit of one and all, then accept it and live up to it."
– Buddha

Thymus Chakra

The thymus chakra is considered a secondary, rather than primary, chakra in the body. However, as we move into a period of awakening of the human spirit, I see the thymus or high heart chakra as a vital part of the full chakra system, of the subtle, spiritual body.

The thymus chakra is often referred to as the high heart chakra or the karmic heart chakra. It is said to be the seat of spiritual development that all soul wisdom passes through. This chakra is all about balance. It is the balance of reason and emotion, related to the heart. It regulates the balance of masculine and feminine energy (every one of us has both). And, of course, it is the balance between health and illness.

The thymus itself regulates the immune system. It helps keep our body's health in check. On an energetic level, it holds the soul memory of the past lives and karmic experiences that we intend to "do over," or try to do better at this time. As our vibration rises to higher levels, we begin to connect to other high-vibration hearts into a collective consciousness of unconditional or divine love. As many of us clear out our karmic baggage of negativity, jealousy, anger, fear, and any other darker ruling emotions, we can realize the connection we have to all other beings on this planet and, perhaps, the universe. Our feelings turn into actions that can hurt or help others. When we fully actualize in unconditional love, we are ready to become one and help others get there too.

Consider how trees live. The study of trees and how they live together and help one another models how people are supposed to live on this planet. When trees grow in a forest or crowded spaces, they create space around themselves to allow others to grow and thrive. They move their branches out of the way for young trees to receive sunlight. They spread their roots out to help their brother and sister trees to get enough nutrients. They even go so far as to share their nutrients with a dying, sick, or fallen tree so that they may heal or feed a new shoot to grow. Trees are truly a collective, helping one another succeed and thrive.

This is what humanity is supposed to be, not the dog-eat-dog approach that most of us have experienced, generation after generation. Balance is what we seek as individuals, but we cannot have balance with ourselves without also having balance with others. Alone and together, masculine and feminine, balance is the task and the solution.

When we find true balance in ourselves, or something close to it, we begin to attract others who are at that same state of being. On a spiritual level, the longing, the aching that we feel to want to be seen and understood is all about finding this balance with our collective tribe. To find that balance, the most important part is self-discovery and self-acceptance. Next is to let go of any and all emotional, mental, physical, and spiritual baggage that is holding us back or keeping us from seeing and loving ourselves. The less we have weighing us down, the more balanced we will be, with ourselves and with others.

The Wisdom of My Being

*I am a product of divine light
and unconditional love.*
*I feel the Divine Feminine
and Divine Masculine flowing.*
*The vibration of the entire universe flows through
my body, mind, and soul.*
*I have access to all the knowledge and wisdom of my
body, the earth, and the universe.*
*With that knowledge and wisdom,
I can heal myself in many ways.*
My soul is my being.
My soul is perfect!
*I free my mind of negative thoughts and relinquish power
from any disease or imbalance in my body.*
*Nothing has power over my body and soul,
except me.*
I choose self-acceptance and love.
*I acknowledge my imbalance, disease, or emotions as an
opportunity
for growth and spiritual education.*
*I know that my soul is infinite in energy and I am always
safe in the divine source of my soul.*
I breathe in love;
I breathe out, I heal with unconditional love.
I breathe in trust;
*I breathe out, I heal with trust in myself
and the universe.*
I breathe in faith;
*I breathe out, I heal with faith in myself, my loved ones, my
doctors, my spirit guides, my guardian angels, and all*

(continued...)

pure, loving beings in the universe.
I am protected.
I am safe in my body.
I am safe in my mind.
I am safe in my soul.

Health

We each must invest in our own well-being. Sometimes we may be sick, depressed, angry, or anxious. Acknowledge that. Accept it for now, only for now. Sometimes we sit with it for so long that it feels like a part of us. The pain, the illness, the abuse, or whatever it is that does not serve our highest good starts to feel comfortable. We begin to have a fear of letting it go, because who would we be then? Each of us deserves to be healthy. Even with a chronic condition, we deserve to feel well most days, right? When we give ourselves permission to be healthy and feel okay, the true self is in balance and harmony in all aspects of health and life. No one is cursed or being punished. We are all worthy of wellness.

Say it:

I am worthy of health.
I give myself permission to feel healthy.
The true, divine me is strong, beautiful, and balanced.
It's time to heal.

Acupressure, Kinesiology, & Tapping for Health

Acupressure, tapping, or EFT, Emotional Freedom Technique, have all become very popular in the last several years. Tapping is not new. It borrows from the acupuncture points in Chinese medicine, stimulating meridians to boost the health and well-being of the body-mind-soul system as well as kinesiology, developed by George Goodhart, DC, in the 1960s. The focus here is on your thymus, for your immune system and your body-mind-soul centering. Tapping or thumping your thymus gland stimulates your immune system. On the physical level, the thymus is part of the lymphatic system. It processes and matures T-cells, which fight and kill off any disease in the body. Stress affects the function of the thymus, which is why stress is such a big factor in our well-being and health. It is a vital gland to our physical and mental health. In theory, tapping this spot on your sternum wakes up or activates the thymus, speeding up the development and release of white blood cells. As this happens, we may feel more energized and revitalized.

Our first point is located on the midline of the sternum (upper chest) at the level of the fourth rib. Activating/tapping this point three times a day helps stimulate healing in the physical body and stimulates the protective immune system functions of the thymus as well as spiritual energetic functions of the high heart chakra. The thymus is located at the center of the breastbone, about four finger widths down from the collarbone. The exact spot is not vital, but you may find it feels like a bruise as you drag a heavy finger up from the center of the breasts. This is a good way to tell you've found it.

The other double point that helps activate this chakra and the immune system is located approximately three or four fingers (width) below the collarbone on either side of the center of your upper chest. There is a slight indentation or sinking down at the point, so if you rub down from the collarbone on either side, you'll find that sunken part. That's the spot! These two points are tapped simultaneously and are known for clearing congestion in the chest or throat. They are also good for slowing down agitated or anxious breathing, as well as regulating thyroid imbalances.

If you're having trouble finding it, Michael Reed Gach, PhD, who has written many books on acupressure, has an easy and loving way to hit both points at the same time. Place your hands over each other on your heart center. The heel of the hand lying on your chest should be dipping down into the space between your breasts. Your index or middle fingers on each hand should be able to touch the spot on your chest that feels a little like an indentation and will likely feel a little sore or bruised. You might need to wiggle your hands a bit or run your fingers along the space to find it, but it is definitely an indentation between two ribs on both sides. Let the tip of your finger press down gently and hold it there for about two to three minutes. Breathe slowly and deeply as you do this. As you breathe and sit quietly, you can repeat:

I am healthy in my body, mind, and soul.

Repeat this about three to four times a day for the best effects. You can also alternate this exercise with a tapping version. Keep your hands uncrossed and find the same spot by placing your index finger at the base of the inner corner of your collarbone, then placing your fingers on your chest, and you'll feel it about three to four finger widths below and one finger width out. Drag your index or middle finger there to tap. As you tap for about 30 seconds to a minute, repeat:

Even though I feel _____ (sick, stressed, anxious, fatigued, etc.), I love and accept myself unconditionally.

You can expand on the statement above, but keep it in the present and keep it simple. Don't worry about what just happened or what may happen in the future. Be right here, right now, holding a space for yourself.

Chapter 10

Throat Chakra:
I Speak My Truth
with Loving Kindness

"When I despair, I remember that all through history the way of truth and love has always won. There have been tyrants and murderers, and for a time they can seem invincible, but in the end they always fall.
Think of it–always."
– Mahatma Gandhi

Throat Chakra

The throat chakra is the fifth primary chakra within the body. It oversees the thyroid and endocrine system as well as our ability to speak up for ourselves—to be seen and heard and express both emotions and creativity, which, in essence, is an expression of our true selves. This chakra resonates in a blue light frequency. When it is in alignment, we speak and express our truth, emotions, needs, and desires with loving kindness and purity. When out of balance, we find ourselves muted, voiceless, with other people not seeming to care about our feelings, opinions, ideas, or needs. It may feel like we are not seen, heard, or matter at all. Health issues can manifest easily in the throat, neck, jaw, and mouth area when this chakra is out of alignment and we are not expressing ourselves as we should.

The fifth dimensional aspect of the throat chakra relates to vibrations and codes of the ancestors of the earth and in the heavens. Powerful healing vibrations, sound and light frequencies, reside, dormant, in our throat chakra. When it is time for all mankind to awaken to this frequency, we will all awaken this healing frequency.

Until then, there are many ways to realign our throat chakras using the power of sound that our own body makes. Singing and vocal warm-ups are a great way to keep the throat chakra in check. A simple lip buzz, hum, or opening the mouth as big as possible, sticking out the tongue and saying "Ahhhh," can work wonders on our throat chakras. Affirmations, chants, and vocal mantras are also an amazing tool; they help many, or sometimes all, of the chakras fall into balance.

How often do we feel like we don't matter and we're not being heard or seen? That is all part of Throat and Solar Plexus Chakras and, together, these two chakras are vital for singing. We must use our core, our lungs, and our vocal cords to sing. It doesn't have to be a full-on Broadway belt, but it is important that we sing our own praises, even if it's in private, in the mirror, alone. We express our fears and doubts and find our confidence when we find and use our voice! Singing is a great way to find our own power and the answers we seek.

I Am My Truth

I release all doubt.
I embrace only truth.
I release all fear and energy of unworthiness;
I am worthy!
I let go of ego;
I am true to myself.
I let go of self-judgment;
I love myself.
I love myself for all that I am,
without judgment or contempt.
There is only love as I see my truth.
I express my truth with every action I take.
I speak my truth with loving kindness.
My voice is kind and loving to my inner child.
I recognize my own divine light and loving soul.
I am perfectly me!

Sound & Voice

Sound has the ability to heal every cell in our bodies. When we use our own bodies to create sound, whether through song, chant, or hum, we resonate internally, sending healing vibrations throughout our bodies and wherever they may be needed.

Sa Ta Na Ma is an ancient Sanskrit mantra or kriya. Sat Nam is the base of the mantra and is loosely translated as "I am that I am" or "I am my truth." A mantra or kriya is a repeated phrase or song that, in essence, is an active or moving meditation utilizing the hands and the voice for self-healing, relaxation, and improving focus. People in India have been practicing it for thousands of years, but in recent years, UCLA and the University of Pennsylvania conducted studies with people with Alzheimer's utilizing this Sa Ta Na Ma meditation or chant as a way to slow down the progression of debilitating symptoms of Alzheimer's disease. The study proved successful and these techniques are being incorporated into many healthcare facilities now.

I have used Sa Ta Na Ma when teaching yoga, particularly when teaching teens how to regulate test stress. I have also utilized sound in my personal life as well. After a very long and difficult labor, my daughter was born by Cesarean section. During labor, I had a flashback of a past life in which I died in childbirth. When the doctor told me my daughter's heart rate was dropping, I said, "Get her out!" The doctor didn't understand the phrase or had never heard it put that way, so I repeated it louder, and we quickly prepped for the operating room.

My daughter was born with the umbilical cord wrapped around her neck twice. After 27 hours of hard labor, surgery, and trauma, I was having trouble connecting to my lower body and my lower chakras. I had a history, up until that point, of seeing a full rainbow of colors whenever I meditated. After the C-section, I could no longer see orange or red for several months, and yellow was only faintly visible in my mind's eye.

I went to an eclectic goddess yoga class. It was part vinyasa flow, part kundalini chant, and there was a percussionist playing live as we did yoga. At one point, we were instructed to sit on our heels, in Thunderbolt Pose, or Vajrasana, facing the wall, and start, at a whisper, saying, "Sat Nam, Sat Nam, Sat Nam…" We got louder as instructed and the drum would match us. As we started shouting the chant at the wall, I felt something deep inside near my C-section scar. I got a little tearful as we softened our voices until we grew silent and then meditated under the teacher's guidance.

Suddenly, I was able to see all the colors. I saw yellow, orange, and red swirling around. I laid my hands on my belly and happy tears ran down my cheeks. At the end of the class, I told the teacher what happened and thanked her profusely. Turned out that she had not been teaching all that long and was very grateful and touched. That class was never offered again and I was and am deeply grateful that everything lined up so I could go and reconnect with my feminine power center through the power of my own voice and Sat Nam. I am all that I am.

For this exercise, we will use Sa Ta Na Ma, because there is a vocal/sound aspect as well as a touch/physical aspect to the practice. There are many interpretations of why or how Sa Ta Na Ma works. It is believed to fulfill all the sounds of life's essence.

Sa means birth, the beginning.

Ta means life, existence.

Na means death, transformation, or change.

Ma means rebirth, regeneration.

Some believe the full life cycle, or beginning to end of the infinity loop, is acknowledged when you utter each sound. Others say that the meaning of each sound is not important but, instead, that 84 pressure points in the mouth are activated through singing, speaking, or whispering the words. Along with the activation of acupressure points in the mouth, there are mudras, or hand positions, that are done with this practice; they are believed to connect and align us to our higher or divine selves.

Sa: Touch the tip of your index finger to the tip of your thumb. It is believed that the Gyan Mudra frees us from limitations by expanding our awareness.

Ta: Touch the tip of your middle finger to the tip of the thumb. This mudra is called Shuni Mudra and is said to bring peace, clarity, and purity of body, mind, and soul.

Na: Touch the tip of the ring finger to the thumb. The Surya Mudra is said to stimulate our vitality, life force, and health.

Ma: For the Buddhi Mudra, touch the tip of the pinky finger to the thumb. It is said that this mudra helps us to be receptive to spiritual communication.

Using the hand mudras in conjunction with the vocal sounds increases blood flow through our sensory and motor pathways in the brain, improving memory and mental balance.

Begin the practice of Sa Ta Na Ma by sitting in a comfortable position with good posture and support. The first time you practice, you will repeat the phrases four times, touching the assigned finger to thumb each time.

Sa Ta Na Ma, spoken in a normal voice; repeated four times.
Sa Ta Na Ma, said in a whisper four times.
Sa Ta Na Ma, said silently eight times.
Sa Ta Na Ma, whispered four times.
Sa Ta Na Ma, is spoken or sung in a normal voice four times.

Take some time to breathe after this and repeat if you like. Doing this every morning can help you feel more alert. At that 3:00pm lull, you can practice this instead of having coffee. You can practice this with your children before they do their homework as well.

Build up your time practicing the mantra-mudra combination. Practice saying it out loud for 30 seconds, whisper for 30 seconds, repeat silently for one minute, whisper for 30 seconds, and end out loud for 30 seconds. When you're ready, you can increase the amount of time to one minute or two minutes each; the point is to do it daily to wake up your brain and you will find yourself more alert and awake, with more focus and memory over time.

As noted, this exercise can be done with children. They love it and it helps with fine-motor skills, coordination, and concentration. The finger touches are great for concentration and coordination. With children, I like to change it up if we're doing multiple rounds. I always start and end with Sa Ta Na Ma and I will add some other four-syllable affirmations to help them with self-confidence and self-love for years to come!

Sa Ta Na Ma
I am okay.
I am enough.
I am worthy.
I am perfect.
I am just me.
I love myself.
Sa Ta Na Ma

Chapter 11

Third Eye Chakra: The Mind's Eye

*"I believe in intuitions and inspirations...
I sometimes FEEL that I am right. I do not
KNOW that I am."*
– Albert Einstein

Third Eye Chakra: Intuition

The third eye chakra is known as the ajna chakra in Sanskrit. Ajna means command and perceiving. This chakra is our mind's eye, where we experience inner vision, dreams, daydreams, imagination, as well as visions beyond this world, body, and life. In yogic traditions, the third eye is the chakra that moves us from the ego, the "I," to the collective or unity that we are all connected to each other as one. When the third eye is fully developed, the constraints of time are removed. We can connect to any time or place in the multiverse. We are without limits, because we have surpassed the ego of the body and the ego/logic brain. When the third eye chakra is activated on a fifth-dimensional level, it represents quantum healing, awakening, and manifestation.

In biological terms, the third eye chakra is related to the pineal gland, which governs the circadian rhythms of sleep and wakefulness. It is also the center of perception of light and states of consciousness, including altered states of consciousness. Many people who seek out awakening through hallucinogenic drugs are using these drugs to open their third eye so as to achieve altered states. Although hallucinogens may be quick and effective, they may or may not have long-term effects. When the third eye is opened through practices such as meditation, yoga, tai chi, Reiki, or some other form of still or moving meditation, the effects are enduring, because of the frequency of use. Like muscle memory in exercise, playing a musical instrument, or riding a bicycle, strengthening the third eye takes practice and dedication.

The Clairs

All of the "clairs" are associated with the third eye:

Clairvoyance is also known as second sight. Those of us who can see the future, spirits, past lives, such as seers, psychics, mediums, Akashic Records guides, shamans, etc.

I see.

Clairaudience is hearing things, voices, sounds, or music. The "little voice" inside us is often clairaudience.

I hear.

Clairsentience is the sensation of something supernatural. Feeling tingles, goosebumps, or temperature changes in the body at the mention of something or the presence of a spirit, ghost, or higher being are signs that your "clair" is sentience.

I feel.

Clairalience is the psychic sense of smell. When we encounter a smell that reminds us of a loved one or a place we remember fondly, that is clairalience. We store scents, sounds, visions, in our memory and this is part of the recall. Many people have this in that subtle or occasional activation, but others receive all or many of their psychic messages in this manner. Some can smell illness, death, or specific fragrances of people, places, or things.

I smell.

Clairgustance is the psychic sense of taste. Remember in the movie *Ratatouille,* when the angry food critic takes a bite of ratatouille and goes back to his childhood, when his mother made him ratatouille, his comfort food? That is a version of clairgustance! Many of us have elements of this, but we don't pay much attention to them or work at developing them. We can develop them. It is possible to develop our psychic abilities, unless we defiantly believe we can't.

I taste.

A way to start is to let go of limiting beliefs and anyone's voices in our head telling us "No!" or "You can't!" as well as our own inner critic's voice telling us we're imposters or it's not possible. There are entire galaxies out in space that we will never see with our naked eye or even a telescope, but they exist; we know and accept this. With a developed third eye, we may actually get to visit these places through our mind-soul's eye.

Claircognizance is the psychic sense of knowing. Many of us have this and don't give it a second thought. Have you ever recalled some knowledge or sensed that you knew or understood something, but had no proof or backup to your knowledge? Later it may be proven true, but you still can't figure out how you knew it. That's how claircognizance works. You can't explain it, but there are things you just know. As the third eye opens, it's like a lens or portal opening up and allowing your all-knowing wisdom to come through. All the knowledge, gifts, and talents from all of our lifetimes as well as spiritual and heavenly or other-worldly wisdom comes into the subconscious and conscious brain through the third eye. We are not born knowing everything. Our divine wisdom or psychic ability trickles in as we grow and experience life. As that happens, we have little "A-ha!" moments. Like a camera lens, it takes adjustments to focus the lens and usually on one thing, time, person, or place at a time.

I know.

Freedom from Limiting Beliefs

I release all negative programming from elders,
teachers, and judgmental people.
I release all old programming that does not align
with who I truly am.
I am sensitive and intuitive.
I embrace my sensitivity and intuition.
I embrace my intensity!
I trust myself.
I trust my intuition and the visions, feelings, and words
I see, feel, and hear.
I trust that when I "just know" something,
that I can confidently have faith in that sensation.
I invite all the clairs to light up within me:
Clairvoyance: May I see all that I need to see.
Clairaudience: May I hear all that I need to hear.
Clairsentience: May I feel all that I need to feel.
Clairalience: May I safely smell all that I need to smell.
Clairgustance: May I taste, beyond the physical,
all I need to taste.
Claircognizance: May I know all that I need to know.
I trust the universe to light my journey,
to guide and comfort me when I am confused or doubtful.
I embrace all my psychic and sensitive gifts.
I enjoy this journey of self-rediscovery.
I love all that I am!

Chapter 12

Crown Chakra: Enlightenment

"People will do anything, no matter how absurd, in order to avoid facing their own souls. One does not become enlightened by imagining figures of light, but by making the darkness conscious."
– Carl Jung, *Psychology and Alchemy*

Crown Chakra: Faith & Enlightenment

The seventh chakra is at the top of the head and is the point of entry for all spiritual information and guidance we receive. It is the subtle body's speaker and receiver for asking questions and receiving answers to and from our spirit guides, guardian angels, and passed-on loved ones. This area of the spiritual body helps us realize that we are a soul in a physical body. It is the enlightenment that there is "more than this," whatever "this" is.

If the crown chakra is out of alignment, weak, or blocked, we are spiritually closed-minded. We mistrust everything and everyone when it comes to spirituality and religion. When the crown chakra is aligned, open, activated, and in harmony with all the other chakras, the earth, and the heavens, we feel a strong sense of trust and faith.

The crown chakra is the tippy-top center of the top of the skull, in the area where a baby's soft spot would be. Babies, infants, toddlers, and even some small children have and maintain a strong connection to the spiritual side of themselves and the spirit world. Many children have stories of "When I was your mommy..." or "When I lived in the mountains..." or chatting with passed-on loved ones and being able to identify and describe them, even though we may not be able to see them. It is not their imagination, though the imagination is part of the intuitive center that is the third eye; it is their very clear and open chakras that help them see, hear, feel, smell, and know that all of the spiritual is absolutely real and true.

By the time the soft spot seals, many children will lose their abilities, because no adults are validating their truth, their experiences. It's unfortunate, because those conscious of their psychic or prophetic abilities in childhood often spend a great deal of their life trying to reconnect to that gift in order to find themselves once again. This is not to say that one needs psychic abilities to live a great life. However, we all have innate intuitive gifts and when we use them regularly, we realized that so many of our worries are not worth our time.

If you recall having any of those psychic experiences as a child, consider yourself validated. Yes! It was real. It is true and you are not crazy. Just as we are all capable and pre-programmed with intuition, you can get it back if you had it when you were a child and "turned it off". Your guides and guardian angels have been waiting for you to say you're ready to turn it "on" again. Have faith! Faith means taking a leap into the unknown because we have a hunch or intuition that everything is going to turn out okay. Unseen things may be unbelievable, but it doesn't mean they're not real.

Taking a Leap of Faith

All human beings spend a tremendous amount of time and energy chasing after things. We chase after wealth. We sometimes chase one another! We search for answers. We look up to the sky for guidance. There's always someone listening to be asked for assistance, guidance, or answers. We are never alone.

"Faith is believing in something when common sense tells us not to." It's one of my favorite lines from the movie *Miracle on 34*[th] *Street* (the original). It is the perfect definition of faith. Most of this book does not ask you to explore the woo-woo, but faith requires trust in some things that are not seen, but felt, known, or recognized as truth without any concrete proof.

We've all grown up reading fairy tales and watching movies that require us to suspend disbelief in order to get through or enjoy them. For this next section, I ask that you keep an open mind and allow yourself to suspend disbelief while doing this exercise. Have faith in your imagination, if not your intuition.

The scientific fact is that our brain functions on a conscious *and* subconscious level. We don't think about breathing; we just breathe. We don't command our heart to beat; it beats all on its own. Our subconscious brain takes care of all the functions that we don't have to worry our conscious or ego mind about.

Our soul works in a similar way. A fraction of our soul inhabits our physical body. Part of the soul is above in the heavens, the universe, or the multiverse. Some is connected to the earth, like roots of a tree, keeping us grounded to the physical world and our soul blueprint (mentioned earlier in the book starting in chapter 1) and karma. The part of our soul in our body is connected to the cosmos, earth, and all the elements and beings who have and still do inhabit the earth.

Dragons are considered mythical creatures, but there are stories all around the world about them. They are actually spiritual, angelic beings that can only be seen by those they are present to help. Dragons are angelic, but they have the elements on their side, so they are able to transmute or transform energy in their own cosmic, magical way. Dragons all reside in the fourth dimension and above, so they are not seen with the naked eye, but with the third eye, the mind's eye. We can sometimes catch a glimpse of them in the periphery, through our physical eyes, but many of us, particularly adults, cannot.

Dragons are masters of the elements. Unlike angels, dragons can move easily through the physical world and manipulate the elements. They also represent transformation, because they can move obstacles out of our way and transmute negative energy into positive. Just like Daenerys was transformed into a queen, a leader through the element of fire, we too can become our truest and most confident selves with the help of dragons. Spirit dragons, of course!

The idea of meeting a spirit dragon face to face is a representation of our physical self meeting our soul self. Dragons are angelic. They are in alignment with our divine vibration or our higher selves. The dragon knows the parts of our soul that live above our heads in the heavens and below the feet in the earth (the elements). They know everything about us. They can help us see the truth, but only if we have faith in ourselves and them.

How to Meet Your Dragon
Tratak (Candle Gazing) Meditation

This particular meditation will help you get in touch with the heavenly side as well as the elemental side of your spiritual self. We will start with the Tratak method of meditation, which is the act of candle gazing or flame gazing from yoga and Indian traditions (dragons not included). Even if you don't believe in dragons, the traditional Tratak practice is said to help with concentration, eye strain, stamina, and memory.

You'll need a candle. If you have pets or young children, use a candle that is in a cup or clear candle holder. You want to be able to see the flame. Set yourself up with the candle at heart-center (chakra) height for the most comfortable session. If you're sitting at a kitchen or dining room table or on a comfy couch with the candle on a snack table, that's a little lower than heart level, but just about perfect. Some people sit on the floor and put the candle on a flat chair or table, but safety and comfort is more important, as this is not strictly a Tratak meditation. Better to be lower than your chest than higher, so that your neck doesn't get strained. You will be here a while, so get some pillows to lean on behind you, and maybe even prop up your head and neck if you feel the need to fully surrender and lean back during the meditation. You may ignore the dragon elements of this meditation if they do not resonate with you, as it's not part of the traditional meditation.

WARNING: This is not recommended for people with schizophrenia, seizure disorders, history of hallucinations, or other psychic imbalances.

You may want to have a timer nearby to help you with this practice at first, but it is not necessary unless you feel more comfortable using one. Only during the first few rounds will there be a need for timing so that you get the most benefit and least strain from the candle gazing.

Sit comfortably in front of a candle. The candle is about arm's length away from you at eye level or below.

Find a comfortable place to rest. Start with your eyes lowered and blink a few times to moisten your eyes.

Breathe in for a count of 4.
Hold your breath for a count of 4.
Exhale for a count of 4.
Hold your breath out for a 4 count.

Stay with this breathing pattern for a few rounds. You can come back to this at any time during the candle gazing if you feel distracted, emotional, or uneasy.

Open the eyes and look toward the flame. Notice it has three zones of color and intensity in it, much like your soul: The middle part of the flame is bright and dense, like your body. The lower part is more transparent and red, purple, or blue, like the colors of the earth. The top part of the flame is wispy and transparent, with a slightly smoky or wavy dispersion of light waves almost absent of any color at all, like the spirit world.

Now, look toward the flame and allow your focal point to be just over the top of the flame without blinking your eyes. Start by trying to do this for a few rounds of breathing. Concentrate on the upper part of the flame, the end of the brightest part, with less focus on the flame itself, but more about the expanded view, more unfocused than focused.

Allow the breath to flow in and out. Imagine the light flowing into you with each inhale. If your eyes start to water and you need to blink, go ahead. Work toward staring over the top of the flame for up to a minute or two.

Now, close your eyes. If you can see the impression of the flame in your mind's eye, gently focus all attention on that image without creating any tension or trying to force it. Surrender and allow. This is a reflection of your own divine light, the eternal flame of your own soul. Hold a space for this soft and gentle concentration without trying to hold the image in your mind. Allow it to fade naturally, returning to the breath whenever you need to rebalance throughout the exercise.

As the image of the flame fades, in the distance, beyond the flame, you see a flash of something, a color, perhaps, in the distance. You may feel a soft and gentle breeze blow across your arms or face.

Be patient and, again, don't force or concentrate too hard. Forcing or concentrating too hard engages the ego brain and keeps you from seeing what is in the spirit world. Surrender your ego; have trust and faith that your own divine light will keep you safe. Feel it shining from deep within your belly, behind your navel. Allow that flame within you to call out your spirit dragon from the shadows.

Take a deep breath and, in your mind, telepathically invite the dragon to come forward to be seen. It may come through visually or through another sense. You may only see a flash of color or feel the warmth or coolness of its presence. Just be. Be with it. Allow your divine light to shine brighter, giving your dragon permission to take a form that is comfortable for you to perceive.

Breathe.

Relax.

Perhaps you can feel or see that the light in you is reflected in the light of the dragon. You are bonded. You are connected. Just like you are connected to all living things on earth, you are also connected to all spiritual beings. This dragon, however, is spiritually bonded to you. This dragon knows everything about the true you. This dragon loves you unconditionally.

Inhale, relax. Exhale, release all disbelief and ego, logic brain restraints and restrictions. Breathe in and allow your right brain to awaken.

- What color is your dragon?
- How big or small is your dragon?
- Is your dragon masculine, feminine, or neutral?
- Ask your dragon for its name.
- Ask your dragon to take any feelings, emotional baggage, or mental clutter that no longer serve your highest good.

Be open and allow your dragon full access to your baggage and shadows. Whatever element your dragon is, it can and will use that to whisk away your woes and worries. With fire, it will burn them away. With air, it will blow them into the wind. With water, it will wash away all your burdens. With earth, it will bury them deep underground. With all of the elements, the dragon wisdom knows that the elements are a method or tool of transmutation. All of the negative will be neutralized or transmuted into positive energy in time. There is no longer any need to carry it or worry.

You now have a connection to your dragon and can call on it whenever you need to. Whenever you need to clear away mental clutter, emotional or karmic baggage, or to assist you when you are spiraling in a negative pattern. Your dragon will be there in spiritual form or in earthly creature form. You must ask for help; because of the laws of free will, we must express our desire for help.

Say farewell for now to your dragon.

Breathe deeply in through your nose.

Exhale through the mouth with dragon force.

Keep your gaze low as you begin to blink your eyes. Open them slowly. Look toward your candle. Take a deep, noisy inhale through your nose and exhale once again, forcefully, in a dragon breath, and blow out your candle.

Bathing in the Healing Light

I release all self-doubt.
I release all limiting beliefs.
I release all shame.
I release all fear.
I quiet the critical voice of lies;
I trust only in the voice of truth.
I open the doors of my soul
and allow pain, grief, and anger
to come out of the shadows into the light
where it will help me grow stronger, braver,
and more confident.
I am safe.
I am surrounded by unconditional love
and divine light.
I am safe and protected.
No harm may come to me in the light.
I am washing away all that no longer serves me
as I accept myself as I am.
Bathing in the healing light of truth and divine light
of unconditional love,
I know that I am perfect as I am.
I am perfectly me.

Expansion & Connection Meditation Drawing on Earth & Heaven Energy

Breathe deeply into the lower belly. Breathe out, let go.

Breathe into the bottom of your lungs.

Breathe out, let go, let everything go.

Breathe into the heart center.

Breathe out, release and let go.

Let go of ego...

Let go of self-judgment...

Only then can you recognize your own divine light...

The source light within you...

[PAUSE]

In your mind, travel down the body to the place where life began...When your navel was the umbilical cord of life force from your mother. If any negative feelings arise from mother baggage, breathe in love and breathe out love...

We have all chosen our mothers for better or for worse and have become who we are, perfectly imperfect now. If you are willing, thank your mother now for the good things she provided or modeled for you. If this is not possible, imagine setting her present self aside and imagine the woman who held you in her womb. It was then and there that she held a space for you to transition from soul to body. She was not the same woman you know now. Hold space for yourself now. Let go of any negative thoughts and feelings you can. They are more hurtful and harmful to you than to her. Let it go, even if it is just for now.

[PAUSE]

Bring your focus to the space of your navel...You may put your hands there if you feel called to. With each breath, go deeper into yourself. Beyond the skin, the muscle, the tissue... Go deep into the light of your soul. Can you see it? Can you feel it? It may start as a soft glow or a sensation of warmth... Or you may feel a wave of peace wash over you...

There it is. That is your source light. The Divine Light that is your soul. The spark that keeps this body alive. Your power source. The perfect you. You are perfect here. You are safe from everything and everyone. No one can hurt you. You are divinely protected and unconditionally loved. Always... Stay with this and bathe in your own light. Feel the purity. Allow yourself to be purified by your own divine light source. You have always had the power to overcome. Surrender...

Expand that light in radiating spirals going deep down into the earth and high up into the heavens. You have access to the energy and wisdom of the entire universe and the celestial bodies. Ask for the guidance you seek. Call out to your higher self, your spirit guides, your guardian angels, and all divine beings to let themselves be known to you.

[PAUSE]

You are connected...

You are balanced...

You are exactly at the perfect time and space in your life...

What comes next? Ask for a sign if you need one, or surrender to your own light and open all your senses, even the invisible senses of clairvoyance, clairaudience, clairsentience... See, hear, feel, smell, taste...know what your next step is...

If the next step is not clear, expand your senses wider and bigger and go deeper within to find your burning desire.

[PAUSE]

Without any ego or earthly greed, ask yourself:

What do I want?

Where do I want to go next?

What is my dream?

Hold the answers it in your mind's eye, your heart, and your soul. Take a picture in your mind of it! Trust and have faith in yourself and your guides that you have the power to make it so. Now breathe yourself back into the present moment.

Breathe in deeply and feel the sensation of the energy field around your skin.

Breathe out, feel your skin.

Breathe in, feel your fingers and toes.

Breathe out, wiggle them.

Scrunch your nose and breathe in.

Drop your jaw, open your mouth wide, and breathe out with an audible sound.

Stretch your arms over your head as you breathe in. Lower them slowly as you breathe out.

Inhale, raise your chin; exhale, lower your chin. Come back to your normal breath without thinking about it. Blink your eyes and, just with your eyes, look up, look down, and look side to side. Feel your body heavy, surrendering to and supported by gravity. You are steady and balanced. You are grounded and safe. You are refreshed and ready to live your best life, manifesting your dreams! Any time you are feeling less-than or disconnected, this is where you can focus all your attention. Namaste.

I Am All That I Am

I am light:
I embrace my sparkle.
I am love:
I embrace my compassion.
I am worthy:
I embrace all of my gifts.
I am enough:
I embrace all that I am!

Affirmation of the Day

After all of the work you've done in this book, now you're ready to continue on your own. You've worked through a lot and you are so much more in tune with your divine self. Unconditional love is becoming more familiar and you know you're worthy of it, giving and receiving. It's time. It's time to trust yourself and your guides and guardian angels and your own higher self to recite the healing messages you need every day. Take them from anywhere in this book or use the following word-find to intuitively create the affirmation you need each day, each week, or as often or infrequently as you choose. It's your choice, your free will in harmony with your divinely guided intuition.

Start right now! You are being divinely guided to the words you need to see and recognize as your truth. The first three words that you see in this word-find become your affirmation. Write them down. These are your truth right now. These are the words you need to see and hear about yourself. This is what you need to focus on, just for today. Make those three words into a mantra for today and any day!

Intuitive Affirmation of the Day

```
U S B F A C O U R A G E O U S F W D N Z L C P S K T
B L O O M I N G S C P R B T T H C A L M B G B E M Y
V I L X R P O W E R F U L O R B O E U Q E Q D X J P
M G D Q N A W I N K U C R M O Q N P W S I L L Y K R
U H W O C S A T E Y N L W I N T N X Z E N O U G H O
X T S B S S O T R U S T I N G S E Z I N Q V P C V T
D Q T Z A I E Y G F Z P M D V B C M Y S B E D U Y E
Y O E R F O T P Y W Y E Z F Q A T H R I V I N G J C
A W A K E N I N G S V A B U S L E E X T R S Z R Y T
M O D W X A J M A G I C A L G O D R Z I Y B R A V E
A R Y Q O T F R C W K E B D R C K E J V A M O C Z D
Z T C D H E A L I N G F X C O N F I D E N T M E Q X
I H A P P Y L P M I Z U Z O U M R Q I C F H B F H S
N Y F L M X I B F J X L U M N A I P V W Y O Q U I E
G C W A Q U V Z L O V E D P D T E E I B P U X L C E
Y L B Y T C E W O K E T Q A E F N R N E M G Y Z E N
X N P F R E E X V A S T L S D Y D F E A W H O P E B
Z E F U K A Z H I A C W B S O U L E P U Z T E U Q D
H E A L I N G O N H O Y C I W Z Y C X T R F I E R Y
U D I Q N U B L G E N E R O U S J T Z I D U N I T Y
B E T S D A Q K X O T Z M N G R A T E F U L D Z S F
E D H O R E S I L I E N T A L O I L P U N I Q U E X
F M F T V J H A Q W N R F T R U E G C L I M B I N G
J K U I P S C R E A T I V E T G M H E A R D Z O R L
M C L G P R E S E N T D K Z I N T U I T I V E F Q M
```

I am _____ ,

I am _____ ,

and I am _____ .

     Repeat your intuitive affirmation for the day or the whole week, but keep saying it to yourself, especially when you feel unworthy or your inner critic gets loud. You may find a new trio of words every day. If you find the same words over and over, it's because that is the word you need to hear about yourself most!

Believe these words; your inner self is screaming to be seen, and your spiritual team wants you to remember who you are. Trust and have faith in you. Attract what you want by putting love out in the world for others to see. Only you can make a change in how the world perceives you by presenting the way **you** see you!

Hold space for your healing and loving yourself a little more each day. Be patient and kind to yourself. You are healing and you are worthy! Namaste.

Resources

No matter where you are in your healing journey, know that you are not alone and there are others like you, that feel like you, and things will get better.

IF YOU ARE IN CRISIS, CALL:
The National Sexual Assault Hotline: 1-800-656-4673 or

The Suicide Prevention Hotline: 1-800-273-TALK (8255).

If you can't bear to speak about it, but prefer to chat online, RAINN (**rainn.org**) has that option!

And **The Trevor Project/Trevor Lifeline** has three options: 1-866-7386. There is also a chat option and you can reach out by text by texting "Start" to 678-678.

There is help and understanding out there.

FOR MORE RESOURCES OR TO DOWNLOAD THE
HOLD SPACE
GUIDED MEDITATION AUDIO FILES,
SCAN THE QR CODE BELOW.

Made in the USA
Columbia, SC
21 June 2021